OLD MAN RIVER & ME

OLD MAN RIVER & ME

ONE MAN'S JOURNEY DOWN THE MIGHTY MISSISSIPPI

MARK A. KNUDSEN

with SHAWN PLANK

RUTLEDGE HILL PRESS®

Nashville, Tennessee

Published by Rutledge Hill Press, 211 Seventh Avenue North, Nashville, Tennessee 37219.

Distributed in Canada by H. B. Fenn & Company, Ltd., 34 Nixon Road, Bolton, Ontario
L7E 1W2.

Distributed in Australia by The Five Mile Press Pty., Ltd., 22 Summit Road, Noble Park,
Victoria 3174.

Distributed in New Zealand by Tandem Press, 2 Rugby Road, Birkenhead, Auckland 10.

Distributed in the United Kingdom by Verulam Publishing, Ltd., 152a Park Street Lane,
Park Street, St. Albans, Hertfordshire AL2 2AU.

Typography by Roger A. DeLiso, Rutledge Hill Press.
Design by Hariette Bateman, Bateman Design, Nashville, Tennessee.
Photography by Mark A. Knudsen

Library of Congress Cataloging-in-Publication Data

Knudsen, Mark A., 1939-
      Old Man River & me : one man's journey down the mighty Mississippi
 / by Mark A. Knudsen with Shawn Plank.
         p.   cm.
      ISBN 1-55853-738-4 (pbk.)
      1. Mississippi River—Description and travel. 2. Knudsen, Mark A., 1939-
—Journeys—Mississippi River. 3. Boats and boating—Mississippi River.
   I. Plank, Shawn, 1964- .   II. Title. III. Title: Old Man River and me.
   F355.K59 1999   98-49762
   917.714'33—dc21   CIP

Printed in the United States of America

1 2 3 4 5 6 7 8 9—03 02 01 00 99

CONTENTS

ACKNOWLEDGMENTS

There are always questions.

What have you learned? Has your life changed as a result? What kind of person does these things? How do you find the time or money? Are you brave or foolhardy? Do you get lonely or frightened? How do you meet people? How do you plan these things?

These are questions that would make another story in itself. They cannot be answered so simply—it is lifetimes in forming the basis of the answers to them all. For those who might be interested, I am accessible, not a recluse. Look in the Des Moines phone book. I'm there.

▼

These odysseys are not solo. There are a few close friends who have given support to these wanderings through the years: my mother, my children, a friend who has held the mirror for me to look in, by phone and in person, along the way.

On this trip, thanks to Wayne Schnider, who was my mentor while building *Dulcinea*. Thanks also to Tom Hawley, the former editor of *The Indianola Record-Herald* (Iowa), who let me write about my Mississippi River trip for his newspaper.

And thanks to the man who was Sancho Panza to my Don Quixote; thanks to my faithful lifeguard Shawn Plank, who never let you know I cannot spell and don't even know a dangling modifier isn't a loosely held tire iron; who sometimes vainly, sometimes heroically, tried to verify my folk tales through scholarly endeavors; who learned to let those various experts of "fact" continue to duke it out for their just reward—a double-dip ice cream cone sprinkled with macadamia nuts with a tassel drizzled down the side.

What fun we had with all those fountains of knowledge! Sometimes you just have to do it yourself, and then you still never quite get it, but the search is fun!

Then there were those along the way who gave their time, sharing their world, their lives, their inner selves; who in fact made this story possible. They are the true centerpiece of the narrative presented, named and unnamed.

Thank you all!

PROLOGUE

"Hey! You the guy I heard of?"

The lockmaster was a tough-looking dude. His arms and shoulders were covered with tattoos, and he had a face that looked like someone had tried to beat a road map into it.

"You been down the river in that?" He pointed at my homemade eighteen-foot long johnboat that was made out of wood and painted yellow. His voice was a combination of disbelief and awe. "Clear down?"

"Yes, I have." Over the past couple of months, I had made a Mississippi River voyage from Minneapolis all the way to the river's mouth, all the way to the river's zero marker near Pilottown, Louisiana. Now I was working my way back up the river to New Orleans to go through a lock that led me to the Intracoastal Waterway. Traveling through the series of canals and bayous in Cajun country was going to be the final leg of my trip.

"I don't know if I'm the one you heard of," I told the lockmaster.

"Yeah, you're the one," he replied. He seemed to be saying, "Who else would it be?"

I guess I didn't realize it at the time but a trip all the way down the Mississippi River in a boat like mine is rare. There are many tales of people who say they went all the way to the end, but those people generally pulled out of the river at New Orleans. To say you've gone all the way to the end of the Mississippi River when you've pulled out at New Orleans is like saying you've gone all the way with a Bourbon Street professional when you've just kissed her on the cheek.

There are a hundred more miles of river between New Orleans and the river's mouth at the Gulf of Mexico. That's not far for a river that runs more than two thousand miles, but it is in those final hundred miles that the river becomes, shall we say, interesting. Or how about life-threatening? Or how about prohibited? (Interesting, life-threatening, prohibited, it was just like going all the way with a Bourbon Street professional.)

The Coast Guard sternly discourages small boats like mine from traveling the final miles of the river. I just thought it was more bureaucratic red tape. I thought this admonition was another of the many ill-devised government restrictions I had heard so much about on the way down the river. Many people I met on my trip made their living on the river. They handled the river fine and even put up with occasional floods. But many of them were drowning in red tape. Government restrictions were often ending or threatening to end a way of life on the river. Self-sufficiency on the river was becoming a thing of the past as huge, faceless corporations took over. Silly and frequently unworkable government rules were tearing apart river communities of individuals dependent on each other and making these same people dependent on distant corporations that didn't have any reason to care about them.

So I gave myself a self-imposed waiver on this Coast Guard warning; I ignored it. But as I learned, there was a very good reason for it. It turns out that the end of the river really is dangerous. The current is strong and unpredictable. Giant ocean ships regularly ply the waters and often don't have much room for error. A boat like mine is like a dragonfly on the water compared to the big ships. And those ships don't bother yielding to dragonflies.

And that was why this tougher-than-nails lockmaster was looking at me with his jaw hanging open. He waved me on through the gates.

"You got more balls than me, bud," he said. "It's dangerous out there. Be careful!"

PART I

THE UPPER MISSISSIPPI

1. *Serendipity*

Watergate Marina is the first full-service marina on the Mississippi River and is just a little bit below Lock and Dam No. 1 in Minneapolis. With little ceremony, my son-in-law, Danny, and a friend of his helped me put my boat in the water. At 3:37 P.M. on September 18, 1993, I pushed away from the dock, and my adventure began.

It was an uneventful first day out to kind of get the feel of it all. My goal for the day was to get to Hastings, Minnesota, about thirty miles and one lock away, yet I didn't know for sure where that day would end or, for that matter, where any one of the days ahead would end. My general goal was Pilottown, a small Louisiana town about a hundred miles below New Orleans and eighteen hundred miles from Watergate Marina.

If I had listened to logic, or the voice of reason in my head, I would have turned around and ended the trip at 3:38 P.M. I was highly energetic when planning the trip, but once I was underway, I had my doubts. Why was I doing this crazy thing? After nearly fifty-five years of life, what led me to take this journey? It wasn't exactly a logical string of events. I wasn't a sailor. Or at least I wasn't when I set out down the river.

By trade, I'm a wood turner. What does a wood turner do? In short, I use a lathe to make a square piece of wood round. Amid the chaos of wood piles in the sawdust-choked air of my shop by my house, I turn balusters, porch columns, newel posts, table legs, candleholders, bowls, and much more. Some of my work can be found around my native Des Moines, Iowa, on houses, in downtown law offices, and in Catholic churches. Some of my stuff has even been on exhibit in art museums.

Wood turning pays the bills. Well, almost. It's practically a hand-to-mouth existence. I'm not really one of those people who defines himself by what he does for a living. Wood turner is but a thin shaving of who I am. I've been a golf course superintendent, a bus driver, an amateur radio builder and operator. I played banjo in dance bands from the time I was nine until my late twenties; I built my own house, including wiring and plumbing; I built and managed a mobile home park; I fed cattle and pulled newborns out of calving cows; I've been a draftsman and an architectural photographer; I've studied ballet; I sewed dresses for my first wife when we were married; I made costumes for dance recitals I was in; I sketch; I paint; and I've been told that I'm a pretty good cook if people stay out of my way. Now I'm a ponytailed artist. But I used to be a straight-edged businessman, a real mover and shaker, including serving as president and board member of the South Des Moines Chamber of Commerce.

Along the way, I had three daughters, now grown. They're all as crazy as I am, only smarter: they make more money than me. I've been divorced and since coming back from the river, I remarried. I have spent my life filling my head, not my bank account. I fill my head with anything and everything. And that seems much more valuable to me.

When I was a child, my mother read me *Compton's Encyclopedia* from A to Z. In the encyclopedia, one subject doesn't necessarily flow naturally into the next: Bach, backgammon, bacon, bacteriology. So maybe it shouldn't be surprising that, as an adult, I have taken the same approach to life. This A-to-Z approach has served me well. I find that I can talk myself into places, getting past barriers and breaking through red tape. And it's not a con job. It's just that I am honest, friendly, and sincerely curious and can talk to anybody because I've done just about everything they have done. If they want to talk about dry cleaning, I can do that, I'm happy to do that.

At the same time, maybe this A-to-Z approach has made it difficult for people to know me. A curator at a museum where I had an exhibit of bowls told me as much: "We can't figure out who you are. We can look at people's artwork and tell you what they are about. They seek out a style and stick with it. But we see your work—some is primitive, some is refined—there is such variety that we have no idea who you are."

In short, what I do is just what I happen to be doing when I wake up that morning. I am not where I started out in life. (And some days, I'm not where I started out that morning.) Some people plan and know exactly what they will be doing today, tomorrow, and on a specific summer's day seventeen years from now. I would rather be surprised at what lies around the corner and accept what life gives me rather than trying to lasso it and force an ill-fitting order to it.

I suppose that's a good attitude for anyone who travels. This journey was not my first. Traveling has been a part of me for most of my life. First with my parents, then some more while raising a family. And now, in my mid-fifties, it returned as a significant part of my life.

The phase of traveling that culminated in the boat trip started in 1989. I took a motorcycle trip from Key West, Florida, to the Northwest Territories in Canada, to the Arctic Ocean at the mouth of the Mackenzie River. My next trip was a wide swing through the southeast and central sector of Australia, then came my Mississippi River sojourn.

For those trips, I didn't make a lot of detailed plans. But I also didn't just rush off into the sunset without my toothbrush. I planned with broad brush strokes, making sure to maintain an intimate connection with my surroundings and not to distance myself from the serendipitous.

I suppose this is why I really made those kinds of trips—for the unexpected. You can follow the tour guidebooks, read the historical markers, and see everything that everyone else sees. But if you travel that way, even if you go thousands of miles, you get nowhere. So much of our lives have been spent learning what other people say is important to know, to see, to remember until we end up being the sum of what others think we should be. As I get older, there is a yearning to decide for myself what is important to know, see, and remember by experiencing life for myself.

So even though on the river I was going where others had gone before through the millennia, this time it was for me, by me. There was no grand purpose of discovery, no "Manifest Destiny." It was just discovery for discovery's sake: to turn over no new rocks, just gaze at the same old rocks; taking more time with each one to feel its texture, feel it with my fingertips, tap it with my fingernails, smell it in the morning air, drop it in my pocket, and sense its presence through the day.

▼

I was finally out on the river. It was real. It was happening. I made my way tentatively through the water. The sky was clear, though ahead of me were wispy clouds. The river was smooth, with a little greenish-gray color and there was a breeze. Going by Saint Paul, the water lost its river smell, giving way to the progress of civilization and smells of sewage and chemicals.

With more confidence, I opened the throttle and went along about 10 mph. That was enough to stay ahead of the towboats but slower than some of the hotshots with their runabouts and 100-horsepower motors hurrying to nowhere special and back again.

It was a beautiful night on the river with the setting sun, geese coming in, night sounds, reflections in the water and a crescent moon just after sunset. Then it hit me: I didn't know my way around the river at night. But two guys, Mike and Dan, from Minneapolis saw my problem, tied their boat to mine, and offered to show me how to guide my way through the darkness. They gave me some pointers and some pleasant conversation before cutting me loose. I followed Mike and Dan a few more miles down the river to Prescott, Wisconsin, at the mouth of the Saint Croix River. They pointed out the city dock where I could stay, and then went up the Saint Croix a few miles to their marina.

As my adrenaline flow eased a bit, I started thinking about the times I was driving to Florida the year before, looking out over the Ohio and Tennessee rivers from the highway bridges, wondering what it would be like to be on the river at night. Now, with a taste of it, I wasn't too fond of it. There is so much you can't see, such as floating trees and other junk in the water that can hurt you. With a big boat, that wouldn't be so bad. But in a little open johnboat, it was a little like David and Goliath. After I got my boat docked and calmed down, the sleeping was not bad. There was a highway bridge on the east and a railroad bridge on the west. But the gentle rocking of the boat finally overpowered all the sounds of civilization.

2. Dulcinea

Throughout the trip, I got a lot of the same response when I told people, like Mike and Dan, about my journey. They were curious. People were always asking questions, as if they planned to make their own trip downriver someday. They always asked about the boat. Had I considered getting a bigger boat? Had I considered canoeing down the river?

Taking a canoe wasn't a choice for me. While I had experience with them and while it would have provided a very intimate way to see and experience the river, the canoe itself would have dominated the trip. It would have become the adventure. On the other hand, a cabin boat would have been comfortable but would also have created a larger distance, real and psychological, between the river and me. It would have had all the conveniences of home, but in such a boat my connection with the river would be analogous to my connection with the road when traveling in a motor home.

What I wanted in a boat was a platform that was reasonably stable. I wanted a craft from which I could view the world as it went by yet be close enough to reach out and touch the river and to be subject to its whims, in a reasonably safe way. I started by taking a safe boating course to learn the necessities of boat handling and the "rules of the road." It was there that I had my first contact with the so-called "Tupperware" sailors—with their suntan slacks, blue blazers with brass buttons, and immaculate boats, whose weekend cruises ended with a rib barbecue.

I fled that scene posthaste and ended up at a riverman's boat store, where I was exposed to some old-time river lore and traditions. Those river men were survivors and students of the river. They had paid their dues and earned their rights. Their reward for their years was that they were still around to talk about it. They also had collected a wealth of wisdom along the way in learning to appreciate the river in all of its moods and fits. Their knowledge was available for those who would bend an ear and take the time to tip back and listen.

The design of the boat was the result of those hours of listening to yarns from the river men. I didn't use any plans to build it, just recollections on the back of an old calendar written with a leaky ballpoint pen and scaled out on a sheet of plywood. I built my own boat. The plywood wasn't fancy and the frame came from oak scraps from the shop floor. Through the summer of 1992 an eighteen-foot, flat-bottom, deep-sided johnboat took shape at the end of my house. It was not pretty with graceful lines, but it was pleasant to look at with functional lines. Finally, in the fall I flowed on a good coat of bright sunflower yellow paint to cover it all up, hiding every one of those eighteen hundred screws so carefully driven by hand with that Yankee spiral-drive screwdriver.

Over the winter I continued planning the trip. I talked more with those river rats, got a radio to communicate with other boats on the river, acquired a compass (not to find the way but to keep track of the river's twists and turns), and got the required safety equipment. Finally, I purchased an eighteen-horsepower, rope-start Johnson motor made the same year I graduated from high school. I was told it was dependable and fixable under the proverbial shade tree.

Coming up with the perfect name for my boat was still vexing, but I gave it time. Finally, it came: *Dulcinea*. The name comes from *Don Quixote*, Miguel de Cervantes' classic novel about a country gentleman who imagines himself to be a noble, romantic knight-errant. Dulcinea is the name he gives to his lady-in-waiting. This plain peasant girl he barely knows is glamorous in his fevered imagination, but she leaves something to be desired in the eyes of others.

Perfect!

3. Red Wing

I awoke the next morning at half past six, feeling more rested than I thought I would, ate a quick breakfast, and wiped off the dew that covered everything. There was no public restroom on the dock, and on that Sunday morning, there were no stores, restaurants, or gas stations open. A bush had to do until better things came along. Soon, I cranked up the motor and was off.

That part of the river had a high bluff on one side. High up there were some of those playhouses of the rich and some ordinary houses of the well-to-do. Right on the edge of the river was a railroad track. The other side of the river was low ground and sand bars. The leaves were starting to turn the yellow of fall and some maples and sumac were getting a red tint. There were places the river was almost calm and others that had pounding waves that broke over the bow of the boat as the wind whipped between the hills. It was brisk. The little thermometer on my coat zipper said fifty degrees. Time to put on my old winter coat. I had planned to start the trip earlier in the year to take advantage of warmer weather, but during the summer of 1993, the river didn't cooperate. Record-breaking floods stopped river traffic on the upper Mississippi and shut down the locks and dams on June 25.

The reasons for closing the river at flood stage were not necessarily what we in the hinterlands would think. There was the danger of high, fast waters, but there was also the concern for damage control. River traffic produced wave action against the levees and flooded buildings and houses. The levees and the buildings might be able to survive the high water, but not the pounding waves from passing boats. The river was down enough by August 22 to open to commercial river traffic again. But even when I left, the water was still high, presenting some challenges. There were fewer places to stop along the way because the flood had washed out some marinas. Lack of business during the flood forced others to shut down. Even sand bars, which could be used to camp on, were under water. Flood damage showed up regularly. Trees were uprooted. Cars were covered with silt.

As I continued down the river, I saw homes wrapped around trees like seed corn sacks on barbed wire. I saw stains on the sides of buildings reaching up to the second story. There were some sportsmen's riverside cabins that had weathered it all stoically. And then there were some that were leaning and damaged. Many of the severely damaged or destroyed cabins had a sense of fatalism about them. There seemed to be a sense that a flood like this would happen at some time or another; it was expected, though not wanted. Nevertheless, it would happen. These homes were built on the river because these people had an intimate, tangible kinship with the river. And so these people prepared for it to happen. When it came, they didn't despair. They just picked up the pieces and went on. These homes were valued by their ability to endure the hardships of rising water.

On the other hand, there were some weekend abodes along the river that had an aura of affluent arrogance. They weren't built there for practical reasons but were there to show off and view the river as though it were a caged animal in a zoo. They were built in the same mentality of excess as the million dollar homes in California that are built directly on the San Andreas Fault.

As insurance companies, the savior of affluence, become more powerful and the government's arms more enveloping, an apathetic attitude of blind safety prevails. It was an attitude that makes people think that milk comes in a plastic jug and meat evolves from a shrink-wrapped rodeo tray. One that makes man think he is the center of the universe, and that nature had better bow down in his presence.

▼

A few miles down the river from Lock and Dam No. 3, I stopped in Red Wing, Minnesota, to get some gas before crossing Lake Pepin just downriver that afternoon. The lake is actually a thirty-four-mile stretch of river that has been widened by a sort of natural dam. Silt and sediment flowing into the river from the Chippewa River formed the dam. At Red Wing Marina, I bought my first ten gallons of gas after traveling about fifty miles. As I was getting ready to leave, a man on the dock called to me.

"It's going to start raining here in an hour or so and it's already raining where you're going, with a good wind out on the lake."

The owners of the marina, Bunny and Randy Trok, invited me in out of the rain. I asked about the sights around town and they volunteered ideas.

"You have a driver's license, don't you?" Randy said.

"Yeah," I replied.

"Here, take our car," Randy said, handing over his keys. "That way, you can see the sights and not get wet out in the rain."

I had just met this guy and he handed over his car keys. How did he know I wasn't going to make off with it? Sure, I had to come back to the marina since my boat and all my supplies were there but was that reason enough for him to trust me?

I think he did it simply because I was on the river. I didn't realize it when I started the trip, but I came to realize that the river is a huge, informal cooperative. River people help other river people. Even though I had not been on the river long, I was already a part of that co-op.

▼

While talking with the Troks about my trip, I mentioned a few things I hoped to see on the river before I was done. Among other things, I wanted to spend some time with a towboat pilot. Well, my wish seemed to be their command. When I got back from town, I found out they had made arrangements for me to do so. At six o'clock in the evening, Ross Marks showed up. He was a youngish-looking, clean-cut man in his working clothes—loafers, jeans, and a sweatshirt with torn off sleeves. Soon we were off in his 850-horsepower office, a smallish boat called a pushboat. I was to spend about three hours with him, which stretched to six hours before we were done.

In his thirty-four years, Ross had been on the river since he was a kid and a pilot for fourteen years. He had been a river pilot, going up and down the Mississippi, spending long periods of time away from home. But he found that life was too hard on his family. He saw that other men on those boats who had been gone from home so much that they no longer had family, or had family in name only. It got to the point for some where the boat was more important than family. Ross wanted no part of that, so he became a pushboat pilot.

Most pushboats are used to take barges out of tows and to put others back. They are also used to move barges around the loading facilities. Ross could do that job, still be out working on the river, and stay close to home and family. Ross said that his was a somewhat protected occupation. You had to know someone or know someone who knew someone to get in it. There were schools where you could learn it, but that was only a shortcut to learning the rules and procedures. Getting the job you wanted was in others' hands. He dreams of having a boat of his own someday, but it's tied up in the politics of getting a fleeting permit that lets you park barges along the riverbank. Like his job, for the permits he has to know the right people. The good ol' boy system could work for you or against you.

It was amazing to watch him push these 35-foot-wide by 150-foot-long barges with such precision. He used river currents and the winds to help move the barges into place. He didn't bump or bang, but just nudged here and there. When I returned to the marina, I had anticipated a wet night out on my boat. But there was a note on the door instructing me to stay in the office and put some cushions on the floor, which I did.

4. Landing 615

Rain kept me in Red Wing a day longer than I planned. After it finally cleared, I left Red Wing and got across Lake Pepin in good shape. Then while preparing for the night, it broke loose and rained again, all night. For the next week, the weather was—how shall we say—challenging? Bracing? Adversarial? Oh, what the heck, it sucked! If it wasn't raining, it was blowing, and sometimes it did both at the same time.

Just as I was about to give up on ever being dry again, I finally got a good day and decided to stop. I pulled in to a marina, appropriately named Landing 615, because it was at mile 614.9, near Guttenberg, Iowa. There were well-weathered wooden docks encircled with seasoned fishing boats and not a plastic yacht in sight. I was greeted with a hearty, "Hi, how ya doin'? Need a hand?"

The place was open for those who needed a place of refuge. There were commercial fishermen, just plain-old fishermen, and the owner, Dirk Kann. Dirk said he got into the business the same way he had gotten into some of his other ventures.

"Just sort of was there at the wrong time and couldn't turn away." Dirk made his investment just before the flood. "Now none of us are trying to break even in this business," he sighed. "We are just trying to cut our losses."

Later that night, Dirk invited me to the home he and his family had carved out on the second floor of an old limestone factory building where workers once made river clam shells into buttons. As we sat looking out over the river, he told me about his work, life, and aspirations, and the kinky roads he had followed in his search. We drank one of his special beers. He belonged to a beer-of-the-month club and received a case of selected beers from around the world each month as a birthday present from his wife.

Dirk's "real job" was owner of Kann Manufacturing, a large supplier of big, metal recycling containers in shopping center parking lots. The company also produced specialized deck boats for big tow companies and commercial fishermen's johnboats. Also, as a personal challenge a few years back, Dirk had redesigned a bicycle into a lighter, stronger, foldable configuration. He got the marketing started and turned it over to a colleague. Then he bought the marina. Despite its problems, he said he didn't regret the investment.

"I'm with an interesting group of people and am providing a service. It's a rewarding feeling at the end of the day," he added.

▼

The next morning, I woke up in the lower level of my "cruise ship." The sun was coming up. Or rather, I had faith that the sun was coming up. The fog was so thick that I had to take it for granted the bow of *Dulcinea* was out there somewhere.

There was much activity on the dock as fishermen prepared to go to a fishing platform anchored just below the dam. Even though you couldn't see the other end of the dock sixty feet away, they were ready to go! This I had to see. What did these guys know that I didn't? Even though you could not see or hear anything on the river, they showed no concern whatsoever. We went out across and upstream at 10 mph. In about five minutes, the boat slowed. Emerging out of the fog, right where it was supposed to be, was the fishing platform.

"How did you do that?" I asked the man who steered the boat.

He shrugged. "You just kind of know after all these years."

5. Connectivity

Later that morning, after the fog burned off and the sun was out in all its splendor, I was back on board *Dulcinea*, heading downriver again. Although there was just a light breeze, it was still too cool to shed my heavy coat. I passed under some high bluffs, and noticed eagles circling on thermals doing acrobatics. Down closer to the water, a pair of ospreys dove for fish. Closer to the waterline, the trees had a grazed look to them. The high water had pruned the lower branches to a uniform height as if cattle had eaten them clean. Channel buoys were pushed against the shore every so often. These floating markers that are used to indicate the navigable part of the river had broken loose during the flood.

I felt I was learning a little more about the river every day. Some of the wing dams were now becoming evident without my having to look them up on my detailed river maps. The dams were built under water near the riverbank to help regulate the river channel and gave their presence away by the ripples I could see in the water. I was just above Dubuque, Iowa, at mile six hundred, where there is a long stretch of river that runs straight east for several miles. The buoys were visible as far as you could see. This was one of those areas of the river people warned me about. It was shallow and wide open, and the water could be dangerous in a moderate wind. But for me, it was fine.

It was not unusual to be headed straight east on the river, nor was it unusual to be going west. What was unusual was to be going south. When you look at a map, the river seems to be going generally south. That's true, but you spend a lot of time going back and forth and sometimes even traveling north for short stretches. Doing some number games in my head told me that the distance from Minneapolis to New Orleans was something like thirteen hundred miles by road. But by river, it was around eighteen hundred miles.

▼

As the sun dipped towards the horizon, there was one more lock to go through before reaching Dubuque. I entered the lock with a pleasure boat and at their request rafted to them rather than tying to one of the lock lines. The skipper of the boat told me that docking in the area was scarce because of extensive flood damage and asked me if I knew where I was going to stay for the night. When I told him I didn't, he offered to help.

"You follow us and you can stay at the yacht club. We'll see you have a place." And that's how I met Lyle and Darlene Christopherson. At the dock, Lyle mentioned he sold lawn care equipment.

"What kind?" I asked.

"The orange ones."

"Jakes."

"How did you know that?"

"Well, I used to use Jacobsen mowers back in the days I worked on a golf course." When I had worked as a golf course superintendent I spent so much time with mowers that I knew many people connected with Jacobsen. We spent the next half hour catching up on old times and asking about old business acquaintances before getting back to the present. It was about suppertime and looked like rain, so I would have had to hurry to cook my dinner over my camping stove.

"You sure you want to do that?" Lyle said. "Come on to the clubhouse. We can eat there and stay comfortable and talk some more."

▼

The next morning, I went to the marina office to ask where I could find an electrical adapter for the cellular phone I carried. Ahead of me, a man was asking where he could get some millwork done. He was trying to find wood to match existing woodwork trim in his house that wasn't available from his normal sources. The people at the marina couldn't help him, but I could. I had a friend I had done business with over the years who had his shop down by the river. And it turned out that the man needing millwork knew where I could take care of my problem.

"Tell you what," he said. "You seem to know what I need. I'll take you where you need to go for your phone problem, if you will help me out with this. Deal?"

"Deal!"

And that's how I met Randy Roos. We went to see my friend Dale at Dubuque Sash and Door, and I showed Randy around the place, looking at all the turn-of-the-century equipment needed to do his job. It also gave me a chance to make a personal contact long overdue.

The river is a common thread that brings people together. If it weren't for being on the river, I probably would have never met Lyle and Darlene or Randy Roos. That wasn't the only time the river brought people into my life with whom I had a connection. I met many people on the river who knew the same people I knew. The meandering river seemed to take loose ends of otherwise disconnected lives and twist them together, connecting people in meaningful ways.

6. Fresh Horses

Later in the day, the sky started clouding over and a chill was in the air. Once again, after a short interlude, the rain was back. I dug out my slicker and pressed on. Fortunately, I wasn't too far from Bellevue, Iowa. One more lock about a mile down and I would be there.

While going through the lock, the reverse gear went out on my old motor. The afternoon was still young, so I hoped there would still be someone in Bellevue who could give me a hand. The people at the marina had a friend who was a mechanic just a few blocks away, but it would take a week for him to get the parts. So I went up the road and bought a new twenty-five-horsepower, electric-start motor from Bob Hutchcroft. As we negotiated the price, I asked Bob about the dangers of hitting some of the junk that I'd seen floating out on the river.

"Yep, it happens," he said. "It's just part of being on the river." And then he added, ominously, "Some of the stuff you see; some you don't. There's one," he said, motioning to a boat sitting just inside the door. "He obviously didn't see it coming."

On the back of the boat that Bob pointed to was a one hundred fifty-plus-horsepower motor with everything below the waterline gone. Completely gone! All that was left was a half-inch driveshaft with a graceful bend to the rear. I wondered, "what a jolting affect that must have had on the pilot."

Bob waved his hand toward a couple of guys in the parking lot. "Why don't you go ask them?"

I went over and asked the pilot about the accident. His answer was surprising. "All I felt was a tick. The engine raced for a split second, then went dead." And with a twisted grin, he added, "That was the quickest ten thousand dollars I ever spent! But never mind, the insurance will pay for most of it—this time."

My new motor was an expense I really didn't need, but at least it wasn't a ten-thousand-dollar expense. Now I would be able to continue down the river, and hopefully be lucky enough to avoid those unseen obstacles that could tear up the new motor.

The next morning around half past eight, the new motor and I were out on the river, trying each other out. What a difference. The most obvious change was that it did not seem like I was at a rock concert any more or in the midst of a squadron of World War II bombers on their way to the Rhineland. The new motor was much quieter, like a swarm of bumblebees. The other difference was the extra seven horsepower at my fingertips. Whoosh! Just the back third of the boat was in water and the wake it left behind was smooth. Now when I wanted to make some time, it was possible. I could even get up to 15 mph!

7. Weathering the Weather

From Bellevue, I made an overnight stop in Le Claire. And the next morning, I set out hoping to make it to Fort Madison, but the wind picked up and I had to make an unexpected, but serendipitous, stop. It was so windy that more water was coming over the bow than I could pump out the back. I tried to continue but soon decided it was foolish to do so. Those "gentle" breezes came at me over a mile or so of water with nothing to break them up, causing the water to build up to two- to six-foot waves.

Ahead was a sandy beach, a rarity along the river during the flood, and a small community beside it. It looked like an ideal place to stop until the winds died down. After tying up, I looked across the road and saw a light blue pole building with a sign that said, Levsen's Organ Builders, Buffalo, Iowa. Here I was in a town just barely large enough to make it on the map and right in front of me was an organ builder. I went in to have a look, living up to my reputation that I know no boundaries. What a surprise. It was a father-and-son business. The father, Rod Levsen, had worked for Wurlitzer before going on his own around 1968. Since then, Levsen's had been building organs that found their way into the world far beyond Iowa's boundaries.

Building organs requires a combination of old-world care and craftsmanship as well as a good knowledge of modern technology, such as fiber optics and digital circuits, way beyond Bach. Rod walked around in suntan pants with a folding rule in his back pocket and an ohmmeter and oscilloscope on the bench.

Rod's son, Rod Jr., took me on an eye-popping tour of electronics and fine cabinet making. He showed me past pipe chests of meticulously fashioned wood and metal pipes. Rod Jr. said they constantly searched for high-quality wood as it is becoming increasingly rare, and they had to forever chase after the latest technology.

This was a business and craft that had to be lived. In addition to keeping up with technology, the organ builders needed to maintain their sensitivity to the subtleties of sound. It was a fine art they practiced here in a light blue pole building near the banks of the Mississippi. It ranked right up there with the elite of any sculptor, painter, or dancer.

▼

By the time the winds had died down and the river calmed, it was late. So I stayed the night in my boat on the river in Buffalo, Iowa. I watched the tows slip by on the far side of the river. In the morning, I watched the sun rise in fire and gold, ate a quick breakfast and left ahead of the predicted winds. Wind, rain, drizzle, fog, and cold had made this a rough trip so far. Yet without these inconveniences, I would have missed so much. The things I would have seen would have been the things everyone sees on bright, sunny days, the stuff of tourist brochures.

As soon as I counted my blessings about seeing interesting sights because of the weather, it started to rain again. It seemed like I was asking for it. This time, I put the top up on my boat for a change and shut the motor off. And yet again, bad weather rewarded me. If it hadn't rained, and I hadn't shut my motor off, I would not have had the pleasant experience of hearing the rain falling on the river, sounding like a deep-fat fryer at McDonald's—a gentle hiss. But then, the rain stopped, the sky cleared, and the wind came up. If it wasn't one thing, it was another.

Ahead was Lock and Dam No. 18, near Gladstone, Illinois. There was construction equipment all around the area and a large crane hung over the chamber. I called on the radio and was told it would be quite some time before I could go through. They suggested I tie up behind the guide wall and wait. They would call when they were ready in maybe an hour or more. I wanted to stay as far ahead of the wind as possible and the hour's delay was not in my favor.

After tying up, I walked to the lock office and asked a worker what was going on. He told me a towboat had rammed the gate during the high water. The big crane, a three-hundred-ton capacity model, was hooked to the end of the gate, taking the load off damaged hinges as they nursed it open and closed. I watched a while then went back and waited my turn. A towboat with twelve barges was also waiting to go through. That meant I would have to wait longer. According to the rules of the river, commercial traffic has priority over pleasure craft like mine.

The wind picked up, and the river wasn't very inviting to my small boat; it only seemed to be getting worse. Now, I would have to wait for the tow to go through and likely face an even choppier, more dangerous river. But the captain of the towboat *Frank P. Harvey* gave me permission to go through ahead of him, unless we could go through together. The lockmaster said we couldn't do that. Under normal conditions, that would be acceptable, but not with high water.

"You still want to wait for the yellow johnboat?" the lockmaster asked the captain on the radio.

"Sure, let him go," the captain said.

As I left the lock, the wind was driving hard and waves started coming over the bow. Out in the channel it seemed like I caught every breath of that wind. Yet, had it not been for the generous captain of the *Frank P. Harvey*, I probably would have faced even worse weather. Although the sky was clear and the sun was shining, the wind was blowing spray over me like rain, running down my neck and blowing up my sleeves. The electric pump was just keeping up with water coming over the bow. Tired and wet, I had had enough. It was too rough. I wondered whether I would even make it to Fort Madison.

8. Retirement Grants

At the end of my strength, when I couldn't take the river's battering anymore, Fort Madison, Iowa, came into view. I looked for the first available place to dock. It was closed because of flooding. But it was sheltered, had a nice place to tie up, and had some flat paving where I could set up the tent. Any port would do in a storm. Maybe morning would be better, I thought. While I was tying up, an older man came by with his hands in his pockets, giving me a careful look. He introduced himself as Mel Grant.

"There's bad weather coming for a day or two," he said. "Why don't you forget about that tent and come over and stay with us; get out of all this. You'll feel better, and we have room."

He told me that it had been lonely on the river that year. Everyone stayed home because of the flooding. He pointed out his digs, a fifty-foot houseboat named the *Poo-Byrd*. It was sitting high and dry on a trailer five feet off the ground and a hundred yards from the riverbank.

"You should have seen it a few weeks ago," he laughed. "Right where it is sitting now was eight feet of water. We were floating then. We just sort of guided it back on the trailer as the water receded."

A couple of early retirees, Mel and Bev Grant got their priorities in order before it was too late. They said that it was no fun to grow up always dreaming of exploring and learning new things, yet having to postpone those adventures for retirement. The Grants' philosophy of life was to eat your dessert first before finishing your vegetables. They made time for adventures and discoveries. He had been a printer in Webster City, in north-central Iowa, most of his life. But they decided the river was where they wanted to be. They bought their old boat and began refitting it from the keel up, as money and time permitted.

The next day, clouds came up again and the wind got even stronger. Mel was right about the weather. There were white caps on the river in the morning and the waves were a formidable size for anyone but the tows. And the wind was even giving tow boats problems. You could see them going downriver at a skewed angle into the wind. It was no day for me to be out there but was a good day to look at Mel's boat. He showed it to me in more detail, and I could tell that he was the "proud father." He wanted me to see the work he'd done rebuilding the twin V-8s, putting in new wiring, plumbing, and remodeling the cabin until it had all the comforts of home.

After breakfast, I decided to stop by the local Sheaffer pen company that was only two hundred yards away. I was a native Iowan writing a native Iowan's story. It seemed only proper to do it with a classy pen manufactured by a native Iowa company and to get it straight from their headquarters. The people at Sheaffer looked at me with curiosity as they listened to my request.

"Well, we only sell through dealers," one employee told me. "You could go downtown...."

"No, you don't understand," I said. "The full meaning would be to get it from the birthing place."

There was some conferring over the phone with several different people. Finally, the employee came back.

"Here is one of our catalogs. If you find something that appeals to you, you can come back tomorrow, and we will see what we can do."

I found a pen that looked durable and nice, too. When I came back the next day, they had the pen for me. They had even engraved it as a special remembrance.

"Let us know how things go," an employee told me.

I had picked up a brochure describing the history of the company the day before. Since I might be using one of these fine Iowa tools, I wanted to fully appreciate the Iowa spirit and history that went into this pen and this company. But I found that Sheaffer was Iowan in history and image only. Through many business buy-outs and mergers, Sheaffer had become an international company to the point that the incorporation papers were filed in Delaware. Delaware! So much for that. I'm sure glad I can live with nostalgia and fantasy where reality leaves off. I used the pen in that spirit, thinking proud thoughts of my home state.

▼

Bev Grant worked at Dave's boat store across town, where I made arrangements to have the required twenty-hour check made on the new motor. While at the boat store, I saw all those accessories that everyone just "needs." Of course, I wasn't interested in such frivolous items, but I couldn't resist a little depth finder that was on sale. I thought it would be interesting to follow what was going on below the surface, not just taking on faith that the channel was a minimum of nine feet deep.

People at the boat store told me that the fuel situation downriver was worse than I had been told because the flooding had shut down or wiped out some marinas along the way. They gave me a list of phone numbers of places to call before heading to Saint Louis and beyond. When I called the numbers, to my surprise, all the places were open. There was no problem, and they were expecting me. However, they warned me to take it easy because the water was still high and treacherous. They also warned that there wouldn't be any bank camping. The riverbanks were either in bad shape or still underwater, and the stretch of river from Louisiana, Missouri, to Cape Girardeau, Missouri, practically the entire "Show Me" state, would be a long, no-nonsense trip with few places to stop for any reason. Just getting through it would be an accomplishment with a boat of my size and limited fuel capacity. The river around Saint Louis consisted mostly of large, commercial traffic and that area was still flooded. No sane man would want to be there overnight. I was told, instead, to get to a place called Hoppie's Marina, about twenty miles south of Saint Louis, where I could safely stay the night.

9. Deep River Dreams

I didn't mind extended stays every now and then. It gave me the opportunity to get close to people. But it also broke the pace of the trip. And once back on the river alone, it made me question my sanity again: What was I doing out here? By myself?

The morning sky was red the next day when I left Fort Madison. The water was choppy and the sky turned gray. But then, the wind shifted and the water calmed. The bluffs along the river are low past Keokuk, Iowa, with its stately homes on the hills. Farther downriver, there were places where the river was straight for five or six miles, and I could see distant towns on the horizon. After a while, the clouds thinned and the sun warmed to the point that I took my coat off for the first time since Minneapolis. It felt good.

Below Quincy, Illinois, there were miles of sandbag dikes built to hold back the high water. Around Hannibal, Missouri, the marinas were all gone, as were trees and river banks, buildings and houses. Parts of the houses were hanging in trees. Other parts were floating in the eddies of the backwaters. Two-by-fours, refrigerators, pieces of furniture, dead animals—it was all out there in the river. Navigation guides, called day marks, that are usually anchored near the bank to indicate the direction of the channel were bent over or missing. Buoys that marked the channel's boundary were washed into the brush, and fishing cabins were mangled. All along the river, there were signs of man trying to rebuild in the wake of nature's wrath. Tons of rock and dirt had been hauled in to rebuild wing dams, dikes, and levees. The U.S. Army Corps of Engineers dumped barge loads of rock along the banks to stabilize them. There was hurried activity all along the way. By our standards, the river had done some serious damage. By nature's standards, it was only a minor adjustment. I looked along the banks and thought of what once was sandy—so beautiful, so peaceful, so loving—torn away in a fury of rage and destruction. I knew time would heal it all.

▼

At a quarter to four, I was at one of my mandatory stops, Two Rivers Marina, across from Louisiana, Missouri. It would be an overnight stay, a fuel stop, and place to rest at the end of a hundred-mile day. Tomorrow would be another milepost, a 124-mile day to Woodland Marina, my last stop before Saint Louis.

"Would you like a covered slip?" Jim, my host at the marina, asked me. "It might rain tonight."

"That would be fine," I said.

Jim had been there for twenty years. When he found out I was from Iowa, the land of tall corn, he gave me a message to pass on to the state's farmers: No-till farming works. Methods to reduce plowing of farm fields has resulted in less soil erosion and less silt coming down the river. "The river was cleaner this year than it had been in the past when we had lesser flooding," he said. "Tell them back home to keep it up. It does help. You are here to see the rewards of your efforts."

My new depth gauge had been giving me funny readings on that leg of the journey, so I asked Jim about it. "Oh, those instructions were written by well-intentioned people. It's just that they aren't on the river with them." As he showed me how to adjust the gadget for use on the Mississippi, he said, "It's different out here in the real world."

▼

A young couple, Len and Chris, who lived in the area and had a boat at the marina, came over as I sorted through the cooler to see what was still good and what needed to go. "Looks like you need some fresh stuff there," Chris said.

"Well, this will have to do until I can get to town at the next stop on down at Woodland," I replied.

"Len's going to the store for us. You want to ride along? Tell you what, I'll start fixing dinner while you're gone. No need for you to bother with that tonight. Be our guest on our boat over there," Chris said. I saw that it was a small pocket cruiser with an already smoking grill on the back.

As Len and I walked through the grocery store, she told me that she had lived here years before. But then, she moved away for the good life. Now, she had moved back with the desire to make this her permanent home. Chris was on the road part of the week with his job and was also looking for a way to stay home all the time. But staying close to the river would mean a cut in income and he wasn't sure he could stand that. Back on their boat, I enjoyed the hot meal and pleasant company. We talked late into the night about their dreams and my trip.

"You know, you are doing what all of us wish we could do," Chris said. "It's a dream many have. We just can't seem to do it."

It wasn't that long ago that I had questioned my sanity for being out on the river. And now, my trip was the object of envy. Or maybe I was just serving as a role model, showing that dreams can be fulfilled. I wished Chris and Len could have been back in Fort Madison to hear the Grants and how they achieved their dreams. They were not that much different from the Grants. Sure, this couple was younger, but in many ways their dream was the same. It was a dream of the river. I wondered how many others like this there would be on the river; people who were bound up with the pressures of everyday life, yet had a dream of the river.

10. Gateway

The next day, on my way to Woodland, a small Missouri community near Saint Charles, the tows were getting larger with thirty or more barges. It was a nondescript day on the river. The weather was not as challenging, and it hadn't rained the night before. The river was calm and the scenery changed in slow motion. Things just slowly unfolded with a few staccato notes thrown in to keep me from falling asleep at the switch.

As I passed a farm with fields running right down to the riverbank, I shut the motor off to listen to the barnyard noises—cows mooing, buckets banging, tractors pulling manure spreaders, dogs barking. For about fifteen minutes, I just drifted, letting the boat pinwheel downstream in the current. I watched and listened to the water, the birds, and the sounds of civilization from over the hill. Sound travels so easily across the water.

▼

Towards late afternoon, the backwater was in view that would lead to the Woodland Marina, a kind of upscale place with big houseboats and luxurious dinghies to float out to them. The marina was open but isolated. The river was six feet above flood stage, and the only road leading there was underwater. The little community of Woodland, just behind the marina, was wiped out in the flood. There was a question, as there was in Niota, whether there would be any rebuilding. Niota was a town in Illinois that Mel took me to witness. It was all but wiped out by the flooding, and the state wouldn't permit rebuilding unless it was to one-hundred-year flood standards. Since many of these river towns were poor, few people, if any, could afford rebuilding. Woodland, however, was an exception. The marina it sat behind catered to some wealthy clientele who brought in the dollars, but they still questioned rebuilding because most people commuted anyway. The large boats there seldom ventured more than a few miles from home—most just went out to a close remote backwater and anchored. There, passengers whiled away the day, and possibly the evening, with beer and barbecue. They returned before the engine oil was even really warmed up good.

▼

It was 7:40 A.M. on a Sunday. It was the day I would go through Saint Louis and all the way to Hoppie's. I'd been told this would be a long day on the river. It was just seventy-five miles, but I expected delays at the locks waiting for commercial traffic. A few miles down was the community of Portage des Sioux, Missouri, the site of some dangerous flooding. Life in Portage des Sioux can be miserable when there is heavy rain on both the Mississippi and Missouri river watersheds because the town is located on the Mississippi near the mouth of the Missouri. Portage des Sioux floods from both east and west as the Missouri River tries to reclaim its ancient riverbed right through the town.

I passed Our Lady of the Rivers Shrine, a fifty-foot statue on a seventeen-foot pedestal built near the river. The shrine was built to thank whoever was in charge upstairs for saving the town from the flood of 1951. But now, in the wake of the flood of 1993, a marina behind the shrine was flooded out. The boats tied to their floating docks were safe, but the office had water going through the second-story windows. Other rooftops were sticking out of the water like grave markers in a memorial garden. Meanwhile, the water lapped at the statue's feet, giving the impression that the Madonna was blessing this flood of 1993, as her uplifted hand pointed across the water.

The water level rose dramatically as I got closer to the mouths of the Missouri River on my right and the Illinois River on my left, each carrying drainage from their namesake states. Barge traffic also picked up, even on a Sunday. There was heavy turbulence in the water as I crossed the mouth of the Illinois River. The waters mixed slowly as the Illinois and Mississippi came together. Just as these waters seemed to come to an agreement with each other, the Missouri came in from the west. Here, there was even more turbulence, followed by a general clouding of the water. It's not called the muddy Missouri for nothing.

A sign reminded all boaters to take the Chain of Rocks Canal above Saint Louis. The eight-mile-long canal is a man-made bypass around the river's Chain of Rocks Reach, a series of natural rock ledges that extend into the river. In the canal, the wind was blocked and the water was smooth. The view of the surrounding country was blocked, too. The canal is just a ditch, which re-enters the Mississippi about three miles above the Gateway Arch in Saint Louis.

At a quarter to twelve, I passed under a highway bridge and then passed the Arch. The Gateway Arch was built in the 1960s as a way to symbolize Saint Louis' role as "Gateway to the West." But for me, it became a symbol of my journey south and into an area different in character from the one I was now leaving. At the end of the Chain of Rocks Canal, I passed through Lock 27, the last one on the river. I had left the upper Mississippi behind. And now the Arch served as my gateway to the lower Mississippi River.

PART II
THE LOWER MISSISSIPPI

1. Hoppie's

There was a gradual transition from the upper to the lower Mississippi. Beyond Lock 27, it becomes a free-running river that stops for nothing until it reaches the Gulf of Mexico. There was an increase in the current visible on the buoys. Faster-moving water piles up about ten inches on the upriver side of the buoy. It formed a wake that I felt in my boat when I crossed it up to fifty feet away. The river also changed from a playground to a blue-collar river. Recreational boaters that were common up north gradually gave way to working boats. I had met at least a dozen tows that day. The previous few days I met just a few in the same amount of time. As I got closer to Hoppie's, I met my first big tow—seven barges wide and seven barges long. That's almost a football field wide and over three football fields long!

Many businesses along the river were gone as a result of the flood, some for good. Others were struggling just to survive. That spirit drew many people together who might not have had much in common under different conditions. It also seemed that their spirit of survival during the recovery made them want to share their otherwise closed society with outsiders. With the high, fast waters, it was not the best time to go down the river. But in terms of human contact, it was a good time. In one way, the river had covered the people who live near it, devastating them. But in another, the river had opened them up and created something new.

▼

Just beyond the tow was Hoppie's, an institution for river travelers. Hoppie's Marina was operated at the time by Charles Hopkins, the third generation of Hopkinses to run a marina in the same location near Kimmswick, Missouri. Hoppie's grandfather, who started the marina, used to row out and light the flame in kerosene navigation buoys at dusk and the business progressed from there through good times and bad. During my journey, the business had been through bad times. During the worst part of the flood, water was a foot deep in Charles' second-story bedroom. Yet, Hoppie's was still open. If towboats had been permitted to operate on the river during this time, the wash they created would have splashed the water up against his bedroom ceiling. I don't think even Hoppie could have survived that. Despite his personal hardships, the marina was open for those who needed him, including the Coast Guard, who depended on him as a fuel stop. He provided a safe haven when others gave up and pulled up the gangplank. Because of the flooding, Hoppie's was the only fuel stop open for a hundred miles in one direction and eighty miles in the other. Hoppie's and a few others were true stoic survivors who made the best of their lot and kept plugging away.

Hoppie's was a place where everything since Day One had been saved and stored in a way probably only Charles Hopkins could understand. In a few acres and old buildings, he saved outboard motors whose nameplates looked more like autographed mementos from the builder than production products. They were kept "just in case." Now they were worth more as collector's items than as a source for spare parts.

Hoppie's old steel floating dock was over two hundred feet long and covered with patina, which gave it character. The patina was laid down by the personality of those who crossed the dock over the years. Hoppie's welcomed many strangers over its ninety-year history who, like me, were just passing through. The docks looked inviting. They didn't ask you to remove your dirty shoes but said, "Just come on in and sit a spell; make yourself comfortable."

Hoppie, a rather shy man with weathered skin and a well-broken-in seed corn cap shading his eyes, looked out for his customers. He did things with a shrug of his stooped shoulders and a casual appearance as if it were no big deal. But his whole operation was marked with his confidence and experience. He was as smart as he was determined. There was nothing but praise about Hoppie on the river. People said that when all else failed, Hoppie was there. He could be counted on when the chips were down. That's why they did business with him and couldn't visualize the river without him.

The night I was at Hoppie's there were river rats, a "Tupperware" yacht, and a thirty-five-foot catamaran tied to the dock. The catamaran was from France on a three-year-plus voyage around the world. Marc Hebert, his wife, and children had crossed the Atlantic and worked their way up from the Gulf of Mexico, entering the Mobile River at Mobile, Alabama. Then, they took the Tenn-Tom Waterway to the Tennessee River, onto the Ohio River and finally, the Mississippi.

Marc and I traded stories that afternoon. He was there by chance rather than plan. He and his family were headed up to Saint Louis but couldn't make it. The river current was too strong for their two small diesels to push against. They had struggled from Cairo, Illinois, where the Ohio enters the Mississippi; the strain proved too great on the engines. They were at Hoppie's to do some replanning and some engine repair. Marc had borrowed a car, driven to Saint Louis for parts, and was now working to put things back in order before going back down the river. Their plan was to go down the east coast of Mexico, through the Panama Canal, across the Pacific toward Japan, down around Singapore, to India, around Africa, and then home.

His preteen children were getting an education they could never have gotten in school. Their school, however, came along on the trip by way of correspondence courses. They picked up the course materials at prearranged post office general delivery points, then mailed them back to France.

Marc and his family, here in middle-America, were exploring a bit of history from their own country. In the early 1700s, the river was a main thoroughfare for French trading, which was admin-istered from offices in New Orleans. This area of the continent was well developed by the French, and there were remnants of that his-tory all up and down the river. Missouri towns along the river like Sainte Genevieve and Kimmswick played a part in French history. Marc suggested that I go see Kimmswick, which was within walking distance of Hoppie's.

▼

Kimmswick was one of those old river towns trying to recover its glory of yesteryear. The streets, however, were not lined with the trappings of yesteryear. They were lined with little places selling blue wooden geese and thorny wreaths more reminiscent of headgear for Easter than door decorations for Christmas. There were places selling snow cones in three flavors and crinkly hard dough sprinkled with powdered sugar. The only place there with history of the forgotten town was the Chamber of Commerce and Historical Society, where I picked up some writings about Kimm-swick's past. The rest was all commercialism riding history's shirt-tails. Other than the written history, the folk tales and a few elderly buildings, the only evidence of real history in Kimmswick was a house built in 1770. It was moved from its old location and turned into a restaurant where I ate.

The real history of the place went to France and then back to me, as related by Marc back on the dock at Hoppie's. It was a colorful history that reminded me of Pasquinel, a character in James Michener's book, *Centennial*. Marc recalled the rugged French frontiersmen and trappers, like Michener's character, who helped create cities such as Saint Louis and Kimmswick along the Mississippi, leaving behind a French influence on what would become America.

2. Forest Kidd

I left Hoppie's the next day for my first full day on the free-flowing river. The water was the color of an old World War I Army trench coat. No matter how hard the cobalt blue sky tried to influence otherwise, the water stayed that same shade of muddy khaki. Along the banks, the trees were changing as I drifted by from hardwoods to willows and cottonwoods. The current toward the center of the river quickened and the eddies at the edge were more pronounced in places. By ten o'clock, my coat was off for only the second time on the trip. The sun had the feel of a warm spring day; a penetrating warmth that felt good all over.

My destination for the day was Kidd Fuel Service at Cape Girardeau, Missouri. It was 106 miles or sixteen pages on my charts. So far on the trip, I had covered about seven hundred miles or 125 chart pages. I was making good time, judging by the regularity of the passing mile makers. It was a good time to shut off the motor, drift like a leaf in the water, and listen to the sounds. At times I could hear traffic from some distant road. Other times I closed my eyes and pictured myself in a hay field, listening to the wind in the grass. When I passed a buoy, the sound of the water rushing by the marker took me to a mountain stream as I imagined sitting beside it listening as it gurgled over rocks. I could hear tractors in farm fields, pulling hard, no doubt working at the fall harvest.

The eddies gripped the boat as I passed, making it sway like a child grabbing a mother's apron strings as she passed. Big tows pushed through out in the channel. I watched them without much concern, as they were out of range. The big standing waves fell behind them for a mile or more, rolling and churning, as if some hidden motor was still there in the river, whirling the water. The churning stirred pieces of trash off the river bottom and brought it floating to the surface, where it sank again. There it waited for another tow to bring it up again, slowly, in that manner, working its way along downstream.

As I approached Cape Girardeau, or "the Cape" as it is referred to locally, I could not only see it, but I smelled it too. It was less than halfway across page 125 of my charts, just above the highway bridge behind a concrete river wall with a mural painted on it. Kidd's, it seemed, was the only thing that remotely resembled a place to tie off, yet there were no signs to identify it and no one around. There was just a rusty, floating dock out there alone tied to the bank somewhere under all that high water. A little cubbyhole of an office out on the dock with the door standing open offered the only welcome. I tied up and climbed up on the dock to have a look around. No sign of life. Around the end of the dock was a floating walk to the riverwall and a set of steel ladders and steps that went over the wall. On the other side, I felt just as alone, in the backyard of some businesses. There was not a sign of life anywhere. Doors were locked, but up on the street level, some thirty odd feet away, there were signs of life, cars, and traffic.

Forest Kidd, I found out, was a petroleum dealer for Sinclair refineries in Cape Girardeau. He would tell you that his was a business, yet like Hoppie, he was there for reasons other than business. Forest did business on his own terms. You bought fuel from him or you didn't stay there. And he was not even at his business all the time. Often you had to go find him. He would turn his back on you and walk away; not with indifference, he would just walk away.

I was told that Kidd was in the second building back up the street. I was also informed that he might not be there, because it was such a fine day. He might have gone golfing, but his man Friday may be around, and if not, there usually was a sign on the door telling when he would return.

There was a sign on the door: "Making a delivery be back about 2." I had about thirty-five minutes to kill, so I walked around town. There were lots of young people: trendy dressers with knapsacks on their backs. Also, there was that Southern twang to most of the voices, not the Northern clip. At two o'clock I went back to see if anyone was around.

Kidd's man Friday was there, but Forest was playing golf and would not be back for another hour. He was the only one who could give the final OK to stay, but since the afternoon was passing, Kidd's man Friday told me to take a chance and plan to stay. It might be OK. *It better be*, I thought, *if I can't stay here, there is no place else.*

"Do you need fuel?" Kidd's man Friday asked. "You have to buy fuel to stay here. I have to leave for another delivery and won't be back till late. Tell you what, you get some fuel and that will give you an in. You just take what you need, fill out the ticket, and wait back up here. I'll leave a note for Forest on his desk and you two can make arrangements when he gets back from his golf game. Fair?" It sounded fine to me.

I sat on his stoop waiting. After a short time the door opened behind me and out came Forest Kidd.

"Hi there! Ya been waitin' long? Just found this note on ma desk, c'mon in, take a seat...see you got your gas already...you be sure you tie up with spring lines, the tows go by close sometimes...where you comin' from...say that's a long ways, we get all kinds here, ya know, some in canoes, some in inner tube rafts, if you're here long enough, you see it all...don't know why I keep this up, no money in it, but someone has to do it or there wouldn't be gas for a hundred miles upstream and a hundred miles south, someone has to be here, don't they?...but you know, it sure is gettin' rough."

"Tell me," I said. "I don't know. What is happening?"

Forest was reluctant, but finally opened up. "Well, I'll tell you. Business is not as fun as it used to be. Too many people trying to get their fingers in where they don't know what they're doing, and too many others in high places who do care, won't tell 'em so."

A growing number of federal rules had made Forest's life harder. As the Environmental Protection Agency and Congress become more sensitive to the wishes of many conservation groups many regulations were pressured through with very little thought about the practicality of carrying them out.

Rules call for anyone holding an inventory of 42,000 gallons of fuel on hand to file a plan for the worst-case scenario in a fuel spill. They also must have a contractor on call twenty-four hours a day to implement the plan. The problem, as Forest saw it, was if he had such a plan in place—at whatever cost—it would take at least thirty minutes to begin the barest methods of cleanup and an hour to start doing any real good. By that time, in the worst-case scenario and a river flowing at eight to ten mph, the spill would be eight to ten miles long and growing.

The only other way he saw to avoid such a problem would be to treat every boat fueling as a potential disaster and completely surround it with a recovery boom before fueling. That would add an expense to commercial boats, which usually fuel up midstream on the go. Now, they would have to stop and possibly separate from their barges and lose time. If that step was required, they would either absorb the cost, or more likely pass it on. The pleasure boater would be out of the game, he speculated. Fueling for just six gallons would be a thirty-minute ordeal that could add $30 to the cost of $7 worth of gas. It could also mean a stretch of river that would have no gas for pleasure boaters. Such rules would also affect Hoppie, meaning there would be no gas on the river for about 260 miles—from 160 miles north of Saint Louis to Hickman, Kentucky.

The next morning I woke up early feeling a little stiff. I was grateful, though, for a place to stay at Forest's. It was a calm morning, one that lends itself to meandering thoughts and reflections, as I made my way to Hickman.

3. River Traits

There is a gradual change from Saint Louis that runs all the way to Cairo, Illinois. Below Saint Louis, the river does not politely succumb to our whims. It does say, "Yes ma'am" and "Yes sir," but more often than not it commands, "Get the hell out of my way!" It also sets the pace of those who live by it and on it. You cannot set your watch to the river for it is constantly changing. Here, the fog, rain, wind, flooding, and currents temper all man's plans—no, dominate is more like it. It is a friendly, yet unforgiving, river. River water is not what you think it is. It is not static, it is not predictable, it does not do what the science books say water does. It does what it wants to do, thank you!

The river was not flat. There were little hills in it and chuckholes. Some were not so little. Some chuckholes I came across were eighteen inches or more deep and anywhere from twenty to one hundred feet across. These were not waves. They were holes in the surface, just like a dip in the road. My boat coasted down one side and pulled up the other. There were places where the current runs back up the river, mostly at the side of the river but not always. And there were eddies that swirled around and around. In places, these eddies turned into whirlpools. The largest one I saw was about eighteen inches across. It had enough power to jerk the boat hard to one side, which was not dangerous to me, but to a swimmer, it would have been the end.

The river also had a crown to it, just like a road. It was generally in the center, though not always. As the river went around a bend, the crown drifted to the outside of the bend. With a little observation, I saw it quite well in a river this size. This was the fast water, right on the top of the ridge, or as close as you can get to it.

The slack water was usually found close to the banks, except on the outside of a river bend. There was a very significant difference in these currents. So much so, that the towboats take advantage of them and follow them as much as they can, not only to gain speed, but more importantly to save fuel going upstream in the back eddies or slack water. For me, I took the fast water when I could; it gave me an advantage of about 1 mile per gallon of gas and a smoother ride.

There were times when the water looked greasy and the boat flew over it with barely a sound, just a hissing and the noise of the motor. Sometimes the wind was so strong it blew the boat upstream along with the surface water. This was the time for small boats like mine to get off the water. Under those conditions waves came over the bow faster than I could pump them out the back.

While the river could produce danger in a flash, it also brought peace and pleasure just as quickly with its sights, smells, and sounds. Two of the beautiful sights on the river were sunsets and sunrises. Cooking breakfast and supper with that backdrop eased the hardships of the day in a big way. Beyond the banks I found some beautiful scenery—little towns tucked in the hills beside the riverbank, and churches in the draws with their steeples peeking at me. North of LaCrosse, Wisconsin, I started seeing ducks in their V formations flying around before heading south. Along with the beautiful scenes offered by nature, there were many unusual things to see on the river. After being on the river for some time, I began to think I had seen it all, but then I was surprised again. In the early morning when I left the Cape, I looked through the mist and saw what looked like a lost Pilgrim boat floating along a short distance behind a towboat. About three hours later, I caught up with it. It was a model of the *Niña*, one of Christopher Columbus' ships, coming down from Chicago on its way to Louisville, Kentucky, for a display.

The river also had many smells—a spring rain, a fishy smell, a musty smell of Grandma's basement, the chemical smell of various businesses, the smell of towns as I approached them, and sometimes the smell of sewage or an oily smell.

Even the sounds of the river were varied and magnificent. They were either subtle or startling. They came in many different tones and tempos ranging from the gentle whisper of water going by to the thrashing of angry water whipped by the wind; from the sound of birds to the rumble of a passing tow; from the buzz of a distant fisherman's outboard motor to the nearby flopping of the big one that got away in the middle of the night. During a rain, when the wind blew, it sounded like someone sweeping dust on a wooden floor. Sometimes I heard a sound resembling a wringer washer—that old sound of the agitator thrashing the water. When the river was angry, all those sounds were present, like a room full of people talking at the same time, yelling and screaming, pounding the table, trying to shout down the opinion of an unpopular speaker. It was a menacing sound I really wasn't happy to hear or comfortable being in the same room with because I didn't know what was going to happen next.

I had two memorable experiences sleeping out in my boat on the riverbanks early in the trip. One was listening to train horns. They were blowing them several miles away and continued blowing them until they just passed by. The tracks followed along both sides of the river. In one particular spot, there were bluffs on both sides. When the train horns sounded and then were quiet, there were pure reverberations up and down the river that sounded like a plucked harp string or a piano note sustained by holding down a pedal. Another time, the night was clear and there was no wind. I lay awake for quite a while, and soon I saw the powerful probing of a tow's searchlight coming my way. As it got closer, I saw the lights on the front of the lead barges and then the lights on the towboat. These were large machines with much power and tonnage, but they slipped by with hardly a sound.

Little by little, I became aware of the unique characteristics of the river. Some would say the river is a dangerous place, and it can be. But it's no more dangerous than the road commuters take to work every day. So far, I had gotten along well. My confidence was up, and I was feeling very self-assured, but I still maintained a healthy respect for the river.

4. Please Forgive Me, Captain

When I took the safe boating course, there was a lot of talk about how dangerous it was to be around large towboats and barges. So far, it had been no problem. But I could see that if a boater had an attitude problem, things could get dicey. It would have been easy to get a false sense of security on the river. There is a big difference between driving a car down the road and a boat on the river. In your car, you can change directions almost instantly. On the river, however, it takes several seconds for a boat to react, so the distance needed to avoid a collision is measured in hundreds of feet or more. It would be easy to wait too long to decide what to do and then when a decision was made not be able to move far enough fast enough. I learned to be careful and that a boater must know his place on the river.

In order to help me make such decisions, I used a radio to call a boat to find out where to pass or be passed. It was a good piece of safety equipment as well as a public relations tool. The other pilots welcomed my interest in their job, my good manners, and my concern for safety on the river. The brief conversations I had with river pilots also led to some interesting talk on side radio channels about things to see and information from their world. I sure learned a lesson the day I traveled from Cape Girardeau, Missouri, to Hickman, Kentucky. I pass it on not only to remind myself but also to alert others who may pass this way.

▼

Just below Cairo, where the Mississippi and the Ohio rivers come together, the river was swift and rising. I had been told when the river was rising to be vigilant for debris washed loose from the banks and the bottom. Debris could consist of anything and was not always floating on top, but could sometimes be just below the surface. I did my best to dodge the trash, which included old refrigerators, dead animals, building pieces, tires, stretches of fence with several posts still hooked together with wire, barrels, and railroad ties. It was all there. Then, I hit something underwater that I could not see. I only felt a slight tug, so I went on not giving it much thought. I should have remembered what happened to the fishing boat up by Bellevue. Sometime later, I looked around sensing something was different, and it sure was! The motor was loose on the transom. No! The motor was not loose; it was tight, but the transom that held the motor in place was loose. The wood had splintered, and it was being held together by its imagination. Previously, the water passing under the back of the boat slipped away smoothly. Now, it arched up just a few inches like a small rooster tail. Something was interrupting the smooth flow of water under the boat.

Without thinking of anything but the condition of the boat, I shut the motor off so I could investigate. The transom seemed tight, and I wasn't sinking. All of a sudden I heard, "Boooooom, boooooom, boooooom…." Looking back toward the sound I saw a tow and a big string of barges that looked like they were headed right down my throat. The tow's horns sounded with real emergency. I forgot about the boat and tried to start the engine without success. There was one of those damn safety locks on the transmission that would not let you start the engine without being in neutral. As the tow moved closer, I could not get it in neutral because there was a bind on the gears.

Quickly, I got on the radio and told the captain what was going on, and he replied he could not stop but would do his best to avoid a collision. He said he was sorry and told me to take care of myself as best I could. A sudden thought flashed through my head: *This is how it ends.* Then I remembered something I was told at Fort

Madison about shorting out the switch. The hood came off that motor like it was never there. As the tow came closer, I fumbled with my pocket knife, touching the metal against what I remembered I was supposed to touch. Nothing happened.

The captain had swung his tow as hard toward the bank as he could trying to miss me and give me as much distance as he could, although if he hit that bank, there would be hell to pay, with barges torn apart and climbing clear up and over the bank. I shorted another screw with my knife, and this time the motor fired. At full throttle, I headed ninety degrees away from the tow, and I got to the side far enough and fast enough that the captain did not have to ditch it. With my heart right behind my teeth, I felt like a fool for stopping in the middle of the channel. I not only gave myself a good scare, but also frightened that captain who was minding his own business when he saw me sitting out there. He had no place to go. He must have had a feeling of helplessness; that he could do nothing all because of my ignorance.

I got on the radio and tried to tell him that I had stopped to look at the damage to my boat and to see what was going on with the motor. There was a long pause on the radio followed by an almost indifferent reply : "Those outboards have a tendency to not be too reliable, don't they?" And the radio was silent.

My adrenaline subsided, and I had more time to think slowly and carefully. What was going through that captain's head? *One more of those amateurs out there. Won't they ever learn. Don't they realize? What is it going to take? You'd think the ones that lose their lives would get their attention. There is only so much I can do in an emergency. Don't they ever just think!*

The river is seductive. It looks so free and open with plenty of so much space for everyone. Even after taking boating courses where much of the time was spent on safety, I still fell short due to my lack of experience. Although the expense can be high, experience is still the best teacher.

▼

In my mind I composed my own boater's apology and plea:

Dear Captain,

I know so little of your world, but I am trying to learn. Will you have patience? I'm sorry for rattling your nerves. Believe me, I wish I had thought. I wish I had known. Little did I realize that although I passed you about an hour before, you were still so close. No, I didn't think I was stopping in the middle of your street. I was only thinking of myself, of my situation. Was I going to sink? Despite the space around me, I should have been respectful of others, of your situation. Now I know better. Forgive me, Captain, and take this as my atonement to you. I pass on this incident here so that others can learn from our fearful experience.

5. The Coast Guard

With time to more calmly and thoroughly examine the damage to *Dulcinea*, I found that the boat was not leaking. The sides were still screwed reasonably tight to the transom, and there was just a little strain. Hickman, Kentucky, was within easy reach, about four or five miles downriver, and the weather was kind. After tying up, I walked through the opening in the riverwall to see what help I could find. I needed some way to get the boat out of the water. I looked for help by the river but was unsuccessful, so I headed toward town. On the way, I passed the Coast Guard station and thought, it couldn't hurt to ask for help there. To my surprise (and to everyone's whom I told the story), they got a truck and trailer and took my boat out of the water. They were not supposed to do that as it was not in their book of regular missions.

After I surveyed the damage, the young Coast Guard man told me he would take me back to their station to decide what to do next. Several others gathered around to examine the boat. They told me there was no one close by to do the work I needed, and there was no way they could take me somewhere to have work done.

"Hey!" I told them. "I built it, I can fix it. I just need a place to do it and a few tools and some other things."

"You sure you can do it?"

"Heck, yes."

"Well, we'll just put you back there in the shade and you can stay with us, it's handy to town and you will be safe here. There is a hardware store a short distance back the way you came."

Stepping into Jack and Helen Gannon's hardware store was like stepping back in time. It seemed more like 1933 than 1993. They had enamel wash basins, coal scuttles on the floor, coal-oil lamps and wick by the foot, everyday-use stoneware, mauls, and splitting wedges. They also had what I needed: screws, a sealant for the joints, and a pilot hole drill. I couldn't find a small container of paint.

"Come here in the back room and we'll see what we can do," Jack said. "Here's an old can, I'll just pour out some, and I'll use the rest sometime."

"I need a hand drill, too," I said, thinking they would surely have an old-fashioned, crank-operated device in such a place. "It's too far to drag an extension cord to where my boat is setting, and I might need it again along the river where there are not plugs by the trees."

"Well, now, I can't help you with that one. We have the electric ones and battery-powered ones, but no hand ones. Haven't had a call for one of those in a long time. What else for you?"

"Well, can you tell me where the lumberyard is?"

"Sure. Why don't I call and they can get what you need ready, then I'll run you up there. No need walking."

He called, but they did not have what I needed.

"No problem, I think Bubba's sawmill surely has that. It's just out of town about eight miles. Helen, will you watch the store while I run him out there?"

And we were off. As we went along, spending a good deal of that afternoon together, Jack was good company, filling me in on the area, its history, and stories of the old days. The story that had the most meaning was of the flooding in the early days. These were people of the river and the river was in them. So when a flood came, there were no vocal cries of despair for someone to come save them from their misery. They just built elevated sidewalks in the street. In the stores, the counters and merchandise were put up and little elevated walkways were constructed with whatever was handy. Business went on till the water went down.

The mill was old, but well-equipped. It was no problem for them to find the little piece of wood I needed, and the work was easy. But at home, getting such a little job done at a big place like that was out of the question. I got my oak and got it cut to size with a bevel and all. I asked about the cost, thinking that cost really wasn't an issue if I wanted to get back in the water. There was about two board feet and twenty minutes of time. Back in Des Moines, I figured the work could have cost twenty dollars, based on hourly rates plus the gouge factor, since it was done for someone in distress with no choice. That's the civilized way in big metropolitan, cosmopolitan, sophisticated centers of commerce.

"Is four dollars too much? After all, it's to help a person out of a scrape isn't it?"

Back at the hardware store, I made a final check over all I needed to repair the boat.

"Here, let me give you a lift back to your boat; save you a little time," Jack said.

By dark, I found all the damage and was ready to fix it in the morning. My Coast Guard friend came over.

"Hey, you look like you could use a shower and a fresh shave. Come on over to the office anytime and help yourself. There's clean towels and whatever you need. No need to rough it by the trees. Make sure you take care of business by ten tonight, that's when we close the doors. We close the gate then too, so if you go to town, make sure you get back in time. Well, have a good night. Your drill will be charged by morning."

In my tent that night, I thought about it all. The river could turn on you at the most unexpected time, but there was a way out, more than a way out. It was a way of meeting people in your life that go the extra mile with you, if you would just show you were willing to go it yourself. There were new experiences, new stories, pieces of lives that came together on the river, all of which were better for having come together.

▼

In the morning, just as I was getting started, Chief Weber, the commander of the Coast Guard headquarters, came by with my drill all charged up.

"How does it look? Think you will be able to fix it?"

"Sure, it's not that bad. Guess I am not as careful as I thought I was, 'cause I sure don't remember seeing anything in the river."

"Well, let me tell you about that," he replied. This was a man who had been on the river all of his life. "You stay out on the river long enough and no matter how good you think you are, things will happen, and those that tell you otherwise are naïve, liars, uninformed, or haven't been on the river much. The river has a way of magnifying life. Don't be fooled by its slow pace. You will experience some of the greatest pleasures of life out there and feel some of life's deepest sorrows, see great beauty and view horror, experience tranquillity and fear. And it will always be that way for those who are on it. Let it show you about life. Never, ever think you have a full knowledge of what's out there because just about the time you do, you will be surprised." As he left, he added, "Let me or my men know if you need anything. This really isn't on our list of missions, so we are feeling our way along with you."

As I worked putting screws in, I thought more about the things the chief had told me. He had once been stuck on the bank, got pushed into the trees, and had the props on his boat tangled with drifting tow rope. These things happened, even to the professionals. It was not much of a comfort, but it did show me that I was not a lone ranger.

6. Reconstruction

After I finally got the sides fastened tight, the next project was to reinforce the area where the motor hung on the transom. To do that, I had to remove the back seat and the fifty screws that held it, put more bracing under it, then put it back. That piece of oak from Bubba's would go across the transom, gluing and screwing all the way. Another half box of two-inch number eights, a little dab of paint, and it would be finished.

A problem arose where I needed a pipe clamp about four feet long to pull a bow out of the transom. I called the hardware store, but Jack said he was out of them. Right across the road from me, though, was a fellow who had a cabinet shop. Jack said his name was Bob, and he was a nice customer of his, so I was on my way over to see if he could help. I didn't even have a chance to cross the road. As soon as I walked back to the boat from the phone, I met Bob.

"Hi! I heard you were here and thought I would just drop by and see how you were doing. My name is Bob Naylor. I have that shop over there," he said, pointing across the road.

"That's a coincidence, I just talked to Jack Gannon. He gave me your name."

"Well, what can I do for you?"

"I need a couple of pipe clamps about four feet long to pull the bow out of this piece."

He was back in a few minutes with the clamps and a first-class battery-powered drill.

"Thought you could use this, too," he said. "I saw what you had and wondered."

He helped me work on the boat and told me his version of history. A real history of the South from a son of the South. Bob told me history as it had been taught to him in Southern schools forty years ago. There are many different views of history. Bob's view was that the North had a stranglehold on the South, that Southerners were denied easy access to manufacturing machinery, and they were relegated to be suppliers of raw materials to the Northern manufacturers. Like the farmers of today, they had little control over prices paid for their crops. The manufacturers seemed to make large profits at the expense of others. In contrast, most of the South was involved in subsistence farming, with farmers just getting by.

Bob came from a Southern family of the area that for generations had been rivermen. He was the one who left to seek his fortune with the chemical industry in the Houston area for twenty-five years. Then one day, the river called him back. I asked him how he had adapted to small-town living after all those years away.

"Well, to live in a small town, you have to get your head in gear, get used to taking substitutes or going somewhere else. Lifestyle is lifestyle, if it's pleasant, that's what is important," he answered.

Bob asked how far down the river I was going. When I mentioned Pilottown, Bob got a steady look in his eyes.

"You know they do things different in that part of the state. Some of the parishes down there conduct themselves like they aren't part of this country. They have their own country and their own ways of doing things. Several years ago, the company I worked for had a dispute with one of the companies they dealt with down there. I was sent down to see what could be done before it became serious. This was in LaFourche Parish. I went down there to see the people involved, and we talked for half a day or more, not getting much of anyplace. It was disturbing to me in that they would talk to me in English but among themselves in Cajun. Finally, I told them it seemed like things were going no place, and I was going back in the morning. The problem would have to be settled elsewhere.

After some talk among themselves, it was suggested we should all think about it overnight and meet again in the morning. The next day, they thought it would be good to go over to the courthouse and talk there.

"Well, what happened was we met in one of the judge's chambers, with one of the judges sitting in, so to speak, as we talked. That was the plan. We should not get into formal court, but just talk it out and see if we could reach some agreeable decision. Then the judge would see if it could be made into an acceptable legal form, typed up, and signed. This, they referred to as 'French Court.' It was approved and settled without formally going to court and that is one of their ways down there still."

Bob and I were doing a lot of talking, but the work was going along at a good pace. It wasn't even eleven in the morning, and I was just about ready to put the finishing touches on, a little quick-set epoxy and an hour later, some paint. While waiting for the epoxy to dry, Bob asked me if I was hungry and gave me directions to a place called Grandma's.

"You go there," he said. "She has our kind of home table food."

There was just a small sign above a steel door in the side of a building. On the other side of that door was a plain room with a mix of furnishings, commercial display tables, old chrome dinettes with matching chairs, and off to one side was a table loaded with food, kind of a cross between a buffet counter and a regular dining room table. There were sweet potatoes, white potatoes, red-eye gravy, green beans with okra and drippings, corn bread, fried chicken, ham hocks, and big jugs of sweet tea. The desserts consisted of bread pudding and thick fruit pies with golden crusts that flake away with the slightest breath. On the table were mustard and ketchup, salt and pepper, vinegar for the greens, and lots of napkins to wipe your fingers and to tuck under your chin. Jack from the hardware store and some of his friends came in as I was looking all this over.

"Come on over with us. We'll show you the ropes."

As the plates were filled and seats were taken, more and more people came in including the banker in his suit with loosened necktie; people in overalls with their pliers in their leather holsters; the seed-corn hat group; and women from the little shops along the street. Off at a corner table, Jack pointed out Grandma, a little lady just a bit past middle age, wearing one of those dresses that my generation called a $2.98 housedress. She looked satisfied with all the activity and showed no signs of weariness from her long days. The conversation was muted and accentuated by the quiet Southern drawl. When I finished, it was time to end it and get back to work.

I picked up a couple of foam brushes and was off. I went back to the boat and finished the painting. Then I looked around the back of the boat to make sure I hadn't missed something. It looked good. All that was left now was to let the paint dry, put the motor back on, and reload the things I had taken out. But I could do that in the morning.

Some of the Coast Guard men and their families were having a picnic near my tent. A young man came over and observed that the boat looked almost done.

"Come on over with us and celebrate your victory. We're having a pig roast and there's plenty. No need for you to eat out of a can tonight," he said.

I joined them at their pig roast and all the high-fat, high-calorie stuff that goes along with it. We traded some old war stories, then I excused myself for one last hot shower and shave. On the way out, the officer for the day stopped me.

"Do you want something to eat? There's plenty."

"Well…no…I think I've had my share for the day," I replied.

"Here, you take this microwave popcorn. You may want some later."

The next morning, it was time to get on the river again. Everyone said their good-byes, and we were on our way to the river with *Dulcinea* on the Coast Guard trailer. By nine in the morning it was travel as usual. Well, almost.

7. Scrap Metal

The landscape was subtly changing. Here and there the mud gave way to a few sandy beaches and the hardwoods were interlaced with cottonwoods. There were fewer bluffs and more miles of levees on both sides, with low, rolling hills behind them. The river changed, too. It was deeper for longer stretches. Instead of the minimum nine-foot channel it was around forty feet deep with some holes up to sixty feet deep. The color of the river changed to a greenish-brown and the current was quite strong, judging by the way the water ran around the buoys.

Around four in the afternoon I got to my destination, a town off the river a few miles called Blytheville, Arkansas. As I was tying the boat off, a man drove up with his wife and family and inquired about my activities. As I told him, a frown came to his face.

"I don't think it's best for you to stay here," he told me. "Why don't you go back up the river where those barges are and pull in behind the second one. When you get there, a tall, thin, colored man named Tiny will no doubt come down and challenge you. You tell him Danny Askue sent you and said it was OK."

So, this is what I did. And Tiny challenged me. When I mentioned Danny, Tiny hesitated, though he finally suggested where to tie the boat and how to tie it for protection from the wash of the towboats. After that was taken care of, I was getting my two-wheeled cart out for the trip to town for gas. Tiny came off the barge he was unloading and informed me it was a long way to town. He asked if I was planning to carry the gas all that way.

Our Lady of the Rivers Shrine was built in gratitude for saving Portage Des Sioux, Missouri, from the flood of 1951. It seems to bless the even more damaging flood of 1993.

In Fort Madison, Iowa, Mel and Bev Grant stand on their boat, Poo-Byrd. *The Grants are a couple who got their priorities in order and achieved their dream of living on the river.*

At Levsen's Organ Builders in Buffalo, Iowa, employee Tim Bovard shows off one of the company's organs, which is made with newfangled electronics and old-world wood craftsmanship.

I'm preparing for the start of my journey in Minneapolis, Minnesota, by moving Dulcinea, *my boat, from its trailer into the Mississippi River.*

In the flood of 1993, high water damaged many of the riverside homes, cabins, and communities along the upper Mississippi River.

Sunrise over the upper Mississippi River.

On the upper Mississippi River near Dubuque, Iowa, a tow appears over the bow of Dulcinea. *Even though the tow was large, it was small compared to massive tows on the lower Mississippi.*

The Mel Price Lock above Saint Louis is the last lock and dam on the Mississippi River. Downstream, the river runs deeper and locks aren't needed to maintain navigable channels.

The view from the river at Saint Louis includes the Gateway Arch and the venerable Admirable *excursion boat (now a gambling boat).*

Steve Stevens' Marina in Natchez, Mississippi, was a longtime landmark on the river. Now, both the dock and Steve Stevens are gone.

Merle was one of the lone, mysterious souls I met along the lower Mississippi River.

"Of course, what's my alternative?" I asked him.

He just smiled and said, "You just waits till I gets done with this barge—'bout an hour on till I gets done—and I take you fo' gas."

It turned out to be twelve miles to town. I got some gas and some new spark plugs. The plugs that came with the motor were the American ones that were recommended by the manufacturer and only lasted about seventy hours. The clerk at the store nodded.

"That's why we don't even stock them," he said. "We only have the Japanese ones."

On the way back, Tiny finished filling me in on what was going on where he worked and back in town. Blytheville was to be one of the major steel towns of the future. A big company with Japanese interests was there making steel I-beams—Nucor-Yamato Steel Company. Other companies were on the way. Tiny worked at an unloading facility for scrap metal started by Elmer Stone and a then-young Danny Askue. It had been twenty-two years since Elmer built his first pushboat in his backyard and hauled it to the river. His had become the major dock and unloading facility for Nucor-Yamato. It was a joint venture with 51 percent American ownership and 49 percent Japanese.

▼

It was a beautiful night and a shame to be sitting behind those barges while a spectacular moon was rising on the mirror-smooth river with tows sliding by on the far side, barely a whisper from their engines. I walked though the yard and found some workers relaxing with a pop. It was the end of their day and things were shutting down till morning and no one was out on the barge they used as a dock. I asked if it would be alright for me to go out there and sit on some of the crates to watch the river for a while. No one seemed to think there was anything wrong with that. I walked out and sat for a while, taking a cellular phone with me for a call back home. What a phone booth! I sat talking and watching the river and the moon and waving to the crews on the passing tows.

Later that evening, probably about eleven o'clock, a vehicle of some kind was driving up and down the road slowly, turning around several times close to my tent. There were voices, of which I couldn't really make anything out except the Southern accent. After a time, they stopped right behind me on the road and were discussing something about that tent down there—my tent. Scenes from the 1960s movie "Easy Rider" popped into my head. And here I was, in the South, in an isolated campsite, a Yankee outsider with long hair, while outside were the sounds of strange Southern men. Needless to say, I was more than a little concerned about the motives and intentions of these strangers outside my tent. As those thoughts of vicious rednecks went through my mind, I wondered, who is prejudging who.

Well, someone had to make the first move, and I thought it might as well be me to get it over with, whatever it was going to be. I opened up the tent and stuck my head out.

"Can I help you?"

"Yeah," one of the voices answered. "Who gave you permission to be here?"

"Danny Askue."

"When?"

"When I got here about four in the afternoon."

"Who told you you could be on the barge?"

"A couple of the workers that were here at about ten tonight when I was there."

"You can't be out there."

"I'm sorry. I did not mean to do anything wrong. I asked before I went out there."

"OK, but you can't be out there—it's not us, it's the insurance. No one can be on those barges unless they work for the company or have written permission."

"Sorry, I meant no harm."

"OK. See you in the morning."

I got back into the tent. I did not need all of that, but it went smoother than I thought it would. As I lay thinking about it all, I knew I had to talk with Danny in the morning. I did not want this to reflect on others who might come behind me looking for shelter. I didn't want him to turn someone away for fear of insurance companies or to think others might do the same thing. I did not have any wrong intentions in mind. I thought I had done what was proper. But I guess there was more to it than even those workers were aware of.

Insurance and the fear of being sued is a real menace to our country. It kills people's desire to be helpful and gives permission for some to be careless and irresponsible. It stops progress by stifling invention and causes inconvenience for some. For example, back in Hickman, Bob Naylor told me of the ferry that no longer runs across the river there. He and many of the residents of Hickman have family and friends that live just on the other side, close enough you could break the sugar bowl in their kitchen window with a .22 rifle. However, the ferry no longer runs. What was once a fifteen-minute ferry ride and a few blocks of driving is now a 115-mile drive. The ferry was a victim of economic times. It wasn't that they weren't making money; they were. It was the boost in insurance rates that forced them to shut down and new government rules that made it impossible to keep running. Insurers and the government were so afraid of something bad happening that they drew up safety rules to protect everyone from every conceivable mishap and jacked up rates to protect the insurance company. It just keeps everyone on edge. And it gives insurance companies huge amounts of control over another person's business and life of which many times the insurance companies have no real knowledge or concern.

The next morning, my first order of business was to hunt up Danny. When I found him, I told him about the happenings of the night before. He just stood there massaging his jaw by pulling on his chin. He looked at me a few seconds and kind of smiled.

"Yeah, I know. I expected I would be seeing you this morning. The boys were around earlier mentioning what happened. They go by the rules. Last night, before I let you stay, I figured you were the kind that would be here like you are now," he said. "That's why I let you stay. Don't worry, you haven't hurt the next one's chances of having a safe place to stay. If anything, you have just given me more faith in my judgment of people. Got to get busy now, you have a safe trip!"

8. Captains

After leaving Blytheville, the river was restful. On the east bank, low hills gradually built for a few miles. At mile marker 780, I found high, steep, and picturesque hills. As I went down the river, the hills were near, then far away, then near, and then far away again. I checked the chart expecting to see the hills represented as a twisted tentacle with numerous, unpredictable bends. But the charts showed the ridge running in almost a straight line. That's when I realized that it wasn't the hills changing directions, it was the river. The bends in the river were very sharp and abrupt. More and more on the radio, I heard the captains talking about upstream traffic and downstream traffic, negotiating it so they didn't meet each other on those bends in the river. There was no room for two-way traffic.

Captains don't have these conversations just before they get to a bend; they inquire about other towboats when they are sometimes five or more miles from the bend. That means they discuss the bends an hour or more before they get there depending if they're upstream or downstream.

▼

Captains live a life most of us couldn't imagine. Their work schedule is grueling both physically and mentally. These men don't have nine to five jobs, nor do they have twelve-hour jobs. They work thirty to forty-five days straight before getting thirty days off. They are on-call twenty-four hours a day, if needed. However, they usually work six hours on and six hours off, around the clock. This is not only the captain's schedule, it is the same for deckhands and mates. There is a psychological factor that must play a number on these men who work on the river, because all the time they are on duty, they are sometimes literally within arm's reach of the bank and could grab a handful of leaves from the pilothouse, but they are not able to set foot on land. These boats do not stop. They are forever on the move or treading water while the tows are being assembled or disassembled. They do not stop for fuel. It is brought to them in midstream by barge and loaded on-the-go, as are all other supplies.

These captains are responsible for everything, including their crew's welfare. This means that the captain must be many things, including a father confessor, confidant, nurse, and referee in times of conflict. The captain is the ultimate authority on all things; the buck stops with him. I'm told these guys get what they want, when they want it. They may want toast to a certain degree of brownness, or eggs to a specified degree of runniness, or coffee as warm as they want it, at any time of the day or night. And they get it.

For all this, they are compensated at rates of up to the range of $100,000-plus per year. Some of the wives of these men wonder if it is worth it. Judging from what I have been told, I think it is not enough. The downside is that many of these men are on their second and third marriages. One woman told me that when these captains are off duty, they want to forget the river, but it is always with them. It is very taxing on the families to have their fathers and husbands away for so long. And when they are home, they want to unwind and don't want to deal with decisions, yet they still have the habit of expecting what they want when they want it.

During their thirty- to forty-five-day stretches, these captains have the weight of the world on their shoulders. There is no such thing as no-fault insurance out here. A mistake is his and the consequences can cause a captain to lose his job forever. His reputation is always in question, and the fines can be astronomical. As captain, he is responsible for the delivery of up to forty barges, each carrying fourteen hundred tons of cargo, which cannot be controlled at the flick of a lever or jerked back in line on a moment's notice. Stopping is measured in miles, not feet. The direction he wants to go isn't determined for the next hundred yards; it has to be planned miles ahead. If a mistake is made lining up for a bridge, the effects can be devastating. Fifty-six thousand tons of cargo can easily snap the concrete support beams of a bridge.

▼

Maneuvering through the bends of the river is not just a case of going around a corner. Keep in mind some of these tows are in excess of a thousand feet long and in a tight bend, it is common for the lead barges to be just clearing the inside bank while the towboat is just clearing the outside bank. In times of high water, tows don't have the problem they do when the water is low. When the bends are very tight, the tows have to be split and be taken around in two sections. This all has to be timed very carefully. In almost all cases, downriver traffic has the right of way because it's more difficult for them to stop and wait, especially in a swift current. These boats need to have headway or steerage, which means they have to be going faster than the current to have active water on their rudder in order to steer the boat and barges. This maneuver is difficult, expensive, and hazardous. Only so much steering can be done with the engines, so downstream boats are usually given favor. Upstream boats can tread water and still have control, so they must wait.

Among the captains, there is a lot of give and take to make life as pleasant, safe, and economical as possible for all, not only in the bends but everywhere. A captain never knows when he will need help. No man is an island unto himself out here on the river. There is a camaraderie on the river that is uncommon in many areas of society. There's a strong connection between these captains. You see it at times where they gather, but most of the time, you hear it on the radio as they talk to each other in their chit-chat and in the business of guiding these monsters on their way. Their conversation is not just polite. It is beyond that. There is a genuine concern for each other's welfare. On the bank, where I have spent all my life, most greetings and well wishes are polite, but insincere. When I drove a school bus some years back, it was customary to wave to each other as we passed on the road. But at other times, most acted as if they never knew each other. That sort of stuff bothers me. I do not like the shallowness of the bankside customs but am leery of the river customs. I want to believe the sincerity of the river, though I'm skeptical because of what I normally live with. But I was treated with great respect out on the river and the rivermen went beyond my expectations. What I have seen and heard is true.

9. Memphis

As I continued down the river, the current changed, the water was deeper, the banks were farther apart, and the people were different in subtle ways. It was a no-nonsense river here. It was not a place for the timid. These river people worked hard and played hard. The poor and wealthy were in it together. They were honest and extremely helpful. And while they were very gracious, they had little time for the pretentious. They respected individuals who did their own thing, no matter how weird they appeared.

There were signs that Memphis was getting close: a few "Tupperware" yachts were on the water, the air smelled like a dentist's office, and it was becoming hazy. I was still fifteen miles from the arched highway bridge that crosses the Mississippi just up the river from Mud Island. The island protects the harbor of the Memphis Yacht Club, where I would spend the night. In the last few miles the sky was really getting an uneasy look to it, the temperature was dropping, and there was a slight breeze blowing, giving me that "look for shelter" feeling.

At the yacht club, I saw a sheet that listed the seniority of the club's members and the waiting list for some of the slips. You would need to sign up as a young man in order to get a slip by the time of your first Social Security check. No kidding! After some checking, I found I could stay if I only stayed until Sunday. I was so beat from the wind and the cold that a room in the nearest reasonable hotel was going to be it for me. The place I found was called River Place. It had once been special but now was a little seedy. I had a spectacular view of the river from my room. I could see Mud Island and the marina where *Dulcinea* was tied up.

As I sat there in the hotel room with the rain coming down, I watched the river shimmer and glisten as the sun peeked through holes in the clouds and danced on the water. This was the same river that jostled me around, made me grow and wonder about the sanity of it all. From here, on the tenth floor and a mile away, it looked so placid, so peaceful.

Just then, the sun came out. I wanted to find a new shirt with big button pockets and all cotton to avoid that slimy polyester feeling, so I went to the front desk and asked about the local shops. The lady at the desk told me there were shops two blocks up and one block down. The stores I looked through were the kind you would find in any downtown area. There were women's stores, men's stores, dime stores, tourist stuff, and a drugstore, but they were all run by and aimed at the black population. When I asked for a shirt with button-down pockets and long sleeves in 100 percent cotton, I was told, "All them stores has moved out east!" I looked around anyway. I saw some real stylish clothes in those black men's stores. And the black businessmen on the streets were really dressed stylish and their suits fit! At home in Des Moines, we have a men's clothing store that advertises: "This suit is eleven years old, a little frayed around the collar, but still in style." There were no eleven-year-old suits here. *There is a lesson to be learned,* I told myself, *when I get home, there are going to be some changes in this honky's wardrobe.*

▼

There was a popular eating spot on the west side of downtown called Cafe Roux, a place where all were welcome, from ladies in black velvet dresses with dangling pearls to those in blue jeans with rings in their ears and tattoos all over; from deck shoes to no shoes, all mingling over Cajun cuisine and breathing fire that peels paint. I was still wearing the same shirt and jeans that I had worn for the past three days, although no one gave it a second thought. No one seemed to give a second thought to the Southern "ladies" chug-a-lugging expensive wine like construction workers drinking beer either.

As strange as this was to me, it was nothing compared to the food—gumbo! Seafood gumbo!

Might as well get with it, I thought, *this is not the North, no sense in having a hamburger.* The gumbo was red beans, rice, spices, and a roux base with a chunk of boudin sausage. They had this green Cajun hot sauce used just like the red stuff only it had a distinctive flavor that eats at you, but doesn't do any harm. To wash it down, being good to myself that night, I had a glass of Folonari Chardonnay and to kill the fire afterwards, a cherry chocolate steamed pudding.

From the cafe, I walked to Beale Street, where it was like Mardi Gras. There was distinctive music in the air coming from one joint after another. Tourists and locals of all persuasions were elbow to elbow. Neon lights hawked for your attention while barkers tried to lure customers inside. This went on for several blocks on both sides of the street and down the middle, where the cars took a chance of being run over by the pedestrians. After taking in as much as I cared for, I wandered uptown toward the famous Peabody hotel, where the genteel have hung out throughout the history of Memphis. Inside there were expensive shops that catered to strained purse strings. There was a designer dress shop, men's clothier selling Armani ties and patent-leather shoes, a salon for manicures, a stationery store with pens loaded with purple and gold ink, and for those with a chill from the air conditioning, a store selling furs.

If by chance you had worked up a sweat from all those decisions, off the lobby in a large sitting room a crystal bar was set up. A large centerpiece was surrounded with finger sandwiches that didn't have enough in them to fill the spaces between your teeth. Behind the table were the bartenders in their stiff white coats and black bow ties. In front of the bar were those same ladies from the Cafe Roux in their black velvet dresses. Men wore Polo shirts and designer jeans if they were "slumming it," or white slacks and blue blazers if they were playing the part of gentility. Here, they did not grip the glass with a closed fist, but held it by three fingers with an arched wrist. The end result was the same, though. They were chug-a-lugging it with shrill laughter and chuckles in place of the "ho hos" over at the Cafe Roux. In my days-old shirt and jeans I was out of place at the Peabody. I was even more out of place than the famous ducks that waddle through the hotel's lobby.

Martin Luther King Jr. had been killed in Memphis twenty-five years earlier, yet it almost seemed that many of these people hadn't heard him or hadn't listened. With the exception of Cafe Roux, the city was segregated based solely on outward appearances. You often find your place in this city based not on the content of your character, but by the color of your skin or by the content of your wardrobe.

10. Yacht Club

Bob Jorgenson had expressed an interest in what I was about; we met at the yacht club. The next day, he showed up and asked me if I would like to see his boat. It was down at the far end of one of the rows of slips. What a boat: it was a steel-hulled houseboat about fifty feet long. He built it himself, and it wasn't the only one he'd built. On the way, he showed me his first one. These were very simple, practical boats made to be safe and do a reliable job with no frills, though they were equipped to provide warm comforts.

After the tour, Bob and I discussed my trip. Others along the way had tried to discourage me from going down the Mississippi below Baton Rouge. The standard arguments were that there was nothing to see but industry, the gas situation was difficult, and the commercial traffic was dangerous. Others told me it would be hard to stay out of the way of the traffic and that the wakes from the big ocean-going boats could be up to six feet high—not something desirable for a small boat such as mine. Bob tried a different tack. He told stories about what there was to see on an alternate route, using the Intracoastal Waterway, a series of manmade canals and natural bayous in Louisiana. They were very convincing stories. Bob said by taking that route, I could see the native Cajun culture that was still intact and enjoy pleasant waterways out of the way of traffic and waves. Plus, I could avoid the smells of the big cities. He had charts he wanted me to take to show the way. I assured Bob I would give his plan some serious consideration. I tucked the charts and his "dreaming book" under my arm, letting him know they would be well cared for and returned.

With those new thoughts in mind, I headed to Mud Island. There is a steamboat museum there and displays depicting the history of the river. I wanted to see a model of the full length of the river from the headwaters at Lake Itasca to the delta below Pilottown. The model is quite large, about two city blocks long, and I spent a couple of hours there reading and taking notes.

The sky had clouded up, promising another rainy night. Rain or no rain, I felt good and rested from a night on clean sheets, so I planned to stay on the boat and get an early start the next day. It was getting dark, so I had to get started cooking. It would be another stew night with carrots, potatoes, celery, onions, a chunked-up can of Spam, salt, and pepper all boiled down as time allowed. If I had known what was in store, I would not have bothered. After downing my supper, I wandered back up to the office to pay the bill so I could leave early. It was Saturday night, but not much was going on. The young man there had his guitar on his lap and feet on a table. He introduced himself as Scott. We began talking about what he had heard about me from some of the regulars who had also heard about me from someone else.

"We get a few through here every year on the way down. Some make it, others don't. How about you?" he asked.

"We'll see, won't we, whether I make it," I replied.

"Tell me, what's your story?" he continued.

"What do you mean?"

"Well, everybody has a story. It seems most who come down here like you are running from something or running to something or just want to get lost for a while."

"Well, I don't know about that. For me, it is an interest in the river and those who are part of it. I guess I never thought of it in that way, but you might have a point there somewhere," I said.

I asked him about his life. He told me he had come from the hills of West Virginia in a log cabin with a dirt floor. His father farmed when he could and his father and grandfather moonshined in between. Scott portrayed his grandfather in bib overalls and a beard to his belt line. By hook and crook, Scott had gone to college and would graduate the next summer. Now he found himself caught in a world of conflict between the world of the hills back home, the song lyrics of his favorite singer, Jimmy Buffett, the college way of life, and what he described as the "abuses of affluences" that he saw among some people. It seemed to me he really did not want to treat life as trivial, something to waste or squander.

On the way back to the boat, I passed by some of the gang that had come back early from the jazz festival in Helena. They had set up a fish fry out on the dock. As I walked by, they hailed me.

"Aren't you the one going down the river in that little yellow boat?" I nodded. "Well, you come on over here and have a good meal before you leave!"

It was one of those invitations I couldn't turn down, even though I had just eaten. It had that tone that it would have been an offense if I did. I swallowed hard. Even though I was flattered to be included into the group, where was I going to put all this food? It wasn't a case of choosing what to eat—a man handed me a plate already piled high with coleslaw, half a dozen hush puppies, shrimp and redfish, with indications there was more to come—heaps of French fries and crappies just waiting to be taken out of the fryer and eaten hot while they are gooood! Oh boy! These guys were all well-lubricated with beer, so I had to be careful. I nibbled and talked and talked and nibbled my way through it all. Then, so I could get an early start the next day, I excused myself and got the Memphis Yacht Club's version of a "Bon Voyage"—slaps on the back and friendly voices telling me to be careful.

"Let us know how it goes, just drop a note to the Yacht Club. It'll get around."

11. Helena, Arkansas

The next day, I was off to Helena, the home of the world-famous jazz festival that had just ended. For me, it looked like an easy eighty miles and one of the better sources of gas on the way down. There were rainbows on the river from some kind of chemical on the surface. This was the location of many of the barge-loading facilities all along the river. Contrary to the traditions of bankside culture, few, if any, of these loading "docks" were identified. On the river charts, they were identified in roundabout ways as grain, petroleum, chemical, cement, etc. They were listed on different pages for specific identifications. And as I found out, they were not always up-to-date, because of all the mergers and selling going on in the business world. There were other explanations for that custom that had to do with a general attitude of not wanting to be all that conspicuous to those who don't know. It would be easy for someone who was not familiar with the river to think there would be no problem with a place to tie up when you looked at charts and saw all the loading facilities. That was not the case most of the time.

The first problem was that not everyone was welcome for various reasons. The other was the physical aspect of it. The docks were strictly designed for loading barges. They were usually a series of large pilings sticking ten to fifteen feet out of the water, placed twenty-five feet or so apart with heavy cushioning material around them such as old, large truck tires stacked like doughnuts or heavy wood timbers held with banding. These were usually in fairly deep water, as these barges are loaded in excess of nine feet of draft. There was no way to safely get from the water level to the top of these pilings. When and if you got up there, there was nothing but large pipes or conveyor equipment and related machinery leading to the bank. All in all, these places are meant for barges, not small boats—not even a good choice in an emergency.

The tows were getting larger as I continued downriver. Some of the larger ones were in the range of forty barges, which were likely built up in a five-by-eight configuration—five barges wide and eight barges long, an area of 175 feet wide by sixteen hundred feet long, or a surface area of more than five acres. A five-acre suburban development has about thirty houses. With the average family size being four people, a tow this size could comfortably hold 120 people with all their stuff.

▼

Helena was a town off the river, behind a little island. It was also a handy town in which to get gas because there was a landing right by the business district, a short haul for my two-wheeled cart. This place must have been jumping over the weekend. The landing was strewn with junk and bottles, and it didn't look good to me. I chose to get some gas and hunt for somewhere else to tie up. After asking around on the other side of the riverwall, I headed off to a gas station eight or ten blocks away. Along the way there was still evidence of a good time by all—booths that were still up and others that were being taken down; discarded programs in the streets and bulletins in the windows of the shops; trash containers overflowing. At the gas station, I picked up one of the local specialties—homemade hot tamales wrapped in corn husks and sold right by the cash register, like sweet rolls and pizza slices are sold back home at the 7-Eleven. Back at the boat, I picked up two more cans to fill and was about to take off when an old Jeep pulled up beside me.

"You goin' for more gas with that thing? We saw you coming back, be glad to help you out."

And this is how I met Chuck and his dad. Dad was a retired chemical worker and Chuck was a crewboat engineer on one of the big crewboats that operate in the Gulf. They drove me up to the station for more gas and got some for themselves. When Chuck went in to pay for theirs, he asked, "Want a tamale? They're a tradition here …"

"No thanks, I already had a couple, but thanks for asking."

When he came back he handed me an Arkansas pin for my hat.

"Something to 'member us by," he said. On parting back at the landing, one of Chuck's last questions was, "You're not planning to tie up here, are you? Better go over there," he said pointing across to a little island. "It might be better."

After juggling my stuff around and filling the boat's fuel tank, I walked back to town on the other side of the riverwall, first taking the time to go through a local museum that gave a good history of the area. It was a story of mostly cotton and hard times, of flooding and slavery, of changes attempted twenty-five years ago with the stroke of a pen in Washington, D.C. Out on the streets, it was more than evident that stroke of a pen could not take away the history of a couple hundred years of antagonism on both sides. The idea was great, but the wounds, real and perceived, were too deep. Maybe in time, but not today.

I headed over to the other side of that little island. It was kind of a city park with a nice observation platform to view the river, where many people had come that day for picnics and just to get away for a while. Toward evening, an older couple came down to where I was to ask about my trip and to admonish me to stay to myself down in these parts, especially from those of the "other race."

Later, toward sundown, the local sheriff and one of his deputies came around. They had heard I was out there and were over checking things out. He assured me everything would be fine. He said he would come around several times during the night and also would turn on the light up the hill, just to make sure. They were careful not to say anything about keeping safe from blacks or people of the "other race." But then they didn't have to.

PART III

MISSISSIPPI

1. Meaning in the Meaningless

I left Helena in the morning. The air was bone-chilling and wind squalls brought water over the bow. Just as fast as a rain storm came up, it was gone. The wind died and the water was calm enough to see your face in. In the middle of the river, a half mile to each bank, there were two monarch butterflies flipping along without a care in the world, just enjoying the moment. It was such a peaceful day that the 130 miles to the marina at Greenville, Mississippi, sailed by without a problem. I called ahead, and they confirmed that I had a place to stay, they had gas, and there would be no problems. I arrived in mid-afternoon, and the opposite happened.

Greenville is not just up a backwater, it is way off the river as it flows today. On the map, it looks like Greenville is on an oxbow of an old flow of the river. But it is a river town nonetheless, with boat building and heavy repair facilities along the banks. It is caught up in the throes of riverboat gambling. They have given over to it, to the point that there is no respectable city dock anymore. *If there ain't big bucks involved*, goes the attitude, *get rid of it*. And that is what happened to the city docks. The marina, or what there was of it, was no better. Contrary to what I had been told on the phone earlier in the day, they had only the very basics. No one seemed to know anything about arrangements for gas, which meant I would have to hunt it up for myself. I was told they had a restroom I could use, though, but the restaurant was not for me.

"It is for more—ah—shall we say—ah, well, ah, you know," my host said, pointing to the well-dressed gambling bunch in their well-padded suits and bulging handbags.

"Yeah, I get it!"

"Oh, it's nine dollars to stay. You can hunt me up in the morning to pay," he added.

Watching from where I was tied, I was entertained that evening by all the lights and hoopla, the bells ringing announcing a winner; the fluff of those just walking aboard and the slumped shoulders of some of those leaving. That went on twenty-four hours a day. The place was not even officially open, I was told. The docks were not complete and there was still work being done to get more glitz on the boat. But the slots were humming, dealers were dealing, and wheels were spinning. Despite the excitement and entertainment, I was able to catch a few winks, so I could get an early jump on the following day.

▼

The next morning I asked some of the early workers where to find a gas station and as I headed out, a young fellow pulled up beside me.

"Say, let me give you a lift. That's not the neighborhood you want to walk through this morning."

So he drove me through a black area that was between the river and the gas station. He spoke in a Southern accent. "This could be a mean town for all. Nobody trusts much of anybody. And as soon as I save a little more money, I'm out of here."

This was his country, and he wanted out. I couldn't blame him. I wanted to leave, too. He dropped me off with my gas and we said our good-byes with friendly handshakes and well wishes. No one was around to take my money at the so-called marina—they were apparently too busy chasing after fool's gold from gamblers. Tourism officials were luring visitors to the river by using the hypnotizing flashing lights of gambling boats. But are the tourists seeing the river, or do they merely have their eyes fixed and dilated on money-devouring slot machines? Back on the river, I was headed to Vicksburg. As I sat there enjoying the natural sights and sounds of the river, I wanted to ask the tourism officials: "Isn't the river enough?"

▼

The river was wide with many islands, some of considerable size. There were many bends and lots of talk on the radio as the pilots set up for their meetings, or more accurately, their lack of meetings, in the bends. When I looked at the river charts, it was evident that there have been many times this river has changed its mind about where it would go to find its way to the Gulf. There were dried-up bends and bends that were still lakes on both sides of the river. More and more, the river exhibited the zigzag course reminiscent of a mountain switchback.

There was not much in the way of things to look at along some of these stretches of the river. I was all hemmed in with levees on both sides. Sometimes there were bluffs to see. Other times I was just in a ditch wondering what was on the other side. There were some good-sized trees along the banks that grew so thick over the years, they gave me the feeling of going through a woods. In most cases, they were second-growth trees that had come up since the levees were built.

Around a sharp bend in the river and up ahead on a bluff, was Vicksburg. As in Greenville, Vicksburg was caught up in riverboat gambling with the competing casino mania. Most of the city docks were again sacrificed for the dollars of the dice, but it was a little better here. The dock was a half mile off the main channel on the way to the Port of Vicksburg. I tied up beside a big jetboat that was used for the tourist trade. That put me far enough away from the floating casino for some quiet and in the shadow of the gambling boat's bright lights for a partially dark night of sleep.

There were many things for the tourist to see in Vicksburg. Civil War history was at every turn. I strolled by myself from the dock up the hill for some window shopping in the folksy part of the town, where the real people lived. I went to Wilson's Furniture and Hardware Store, the pride and joy of Jim and Betty Wilson. The store was founded in 1897 and had been in the same family since then. Each new owner just grew up in it, inheriting the business like one inherits their genes. In that store, I doubt that there would have been another way to do it.

There were no computers to keep track of inventory and no worry if a particular item didn't sell but once a year. It was there to meet someone's need, never mind how insignificant. All the merchandise was handily displayed where you could easily get to it, in those little glass cubes of five-and-dime store history, with the price on a card behind it. Other merchandise hung from the ceiling or on hooks in the wall, piled under the counters, and on shelves. Only a few items, such as pocket knives, were in glass cases with sliding, locked doors. But the keys were hanging on a nail next to the case. In 1936, the store expanded, adding furniture. And when I visited, the 1936 style was the in thing at the store: iron beds, chifforobes, comfortable (if not a bit stylish) chairs, and parlor stoves of the Warm Morning brand-style and the cast-iron variety with a little chrome on them.

Jim and his wife were not that many years from wanting to retire (though they were beyond the magic age of sixty-five) and turn the business over to someone else. But their kids were not interested and no one else had given the store serious consideration. It seemed that others thought it was an unimportant job without rewards—just clerking. I looked around at the stuff they had to sell, some of it to meet modern demands of life and some to meet a slower, older way. These were things like meat saws, flue dampers, a blue stove pipe, stoneware crocks and cast-iron cookware sitting beside the blue enamel kind; galvanized oval wash tubs to take a Saturday night bath in, butter churns, Aladdin lamps, rubber sink stoppers with a chain, white porcelain light bulb fixtures, tire patch kits for tube tires and tire pumps and bins of bolts and nails. Hanging high on the wall were three sizes of washboards and strap hinges for a farm gate. The list went on and on. Where in the world could a person find a job where they could be more helpful to their neighbors? And what was more important than that?

▼

On my walk back through town, I went past the courthouse that sat up on a hill with a low masonry wall beside the sidewalk. It was an old-time courthouse that was all lit up but closed. I wanted to walk around it and maybe look in the windows. When I came to the steps and the walk that led up to it, however, there was an iron gate blocking the way. You could not even get on the grounds. But what really caught my attention was how the gate was secured. It was not a tumbler lock built into the gate. No sir, it was locked with a chain and a padlock, and I mean a big chain that a crane might lift a car with. The links were five-sixteenths of an inch in diameter, and the lock was not one of those wimpy layered Master Locks. It was one of those that let you know the gate was locked. It could have been used to secure Fort Knox. Why had they done this? It was overkill by reasonable standards, but who was I to question? They knew their locks better than I did, what with them still having chain gangs and all.

Although I couldn't get in to see the courthouse, I sat on the hill for a while. The view from the hill was beautiful. I could see the river from where I was, and the sun started to go down. I sat for the duration of this magnificent moving art and watched the brilliant colors slowly swirl and melt from orange to red to black. After the show, I went back down the hill to the boat, had a look around, unrolled the sleeping bag, and called it quits for the day.

2. Supply on Demand

The next day, I found out there was a store nearby, Ergon General Store, that supplied a lot of the working boats on the river. Ergon had everything the towboats needed to keep going, from their mechanical needs to their personal needs. They had everything from pharmaceuticals to groceries and toiletries to hardware. They listed 1,139 grocery items which they had on hand and could fill special orders with twenty-four hours' notice. The meat was all prime grade, cut to order on the premises, including stuffed pork chops, brisket, rolled roasts, and a large variety of gourmet sausages. There was poultry and not just chicken and turkey, but Cornish hens, duck, and quail. The fish included everything from farm-raised catfish to shrimp, to trout and different varieties of whitefish to lobster and crab, if the budget would stand it. The breads, all fresh-baked daily, included white, whole wheat, hard rolls, sesame-seed buns, several types of rye, hot dog buns, and if the boats' cooks were inclined to bake their own, they had all the ingredients found in the best stores. They had cheese, milk, and sixteen flavors of ice cream, a complete line of spices, dried fruits, fresh produce from parsley to potatoes, and the very latest in dry breakfast cereal.

"The men on these boats," I was told, "are like children. They want the newest cereals as well as the old standbys of oatmeal and Cap'n Crunch."

To prepare all the goodies they had commercial grades of all the utensils you could imagine, be it a garlic press or an omelet pan, food processor, or a tea strainer, even a hard-boiled egg cutter. They also had brooms and mops, garbage bags, and soap.

In the hardware end of the store, the list was just as endless. There were all the needs to keep the boat well, healthy, and clean— all the bolts, and cotter keys, needlenose pliers, four-foot pipe wrenches, wire rope, life vests, bright and clean American flags, paint and solvents, oil filters, hose clamps, tow ropes of up to two inches in diameter in six hundred-foot rolls, and much, much more. The orders were sent to the store by radio, by cellular phone, and by fax.

Patsy, the grocery clerk, and Bill Parker, the meat cutter, filled me in on their business and on other aspects of river life. They told me that a boat with an average eight-member crew spends about five to seven hundred dollars per week on food alone. In addition to the crew, each boat has a cook. On the river, men and women both fill this important role. When men serve as cooks, it is treated just like any other job on the boat and these cooks are similar in age and lifestyle with their crewmates. But the women who serve as cooks tend to be older with their children gone. Few are married. I'm told that crews prefer women cooks to men. The male cooks tend to stick closely to a meat, potato, and grease menu, while women simply cook better food. In addition, these women often serve as a mother figure.

The cooks have long hours that start at three in the morning to prepare breakfast. After cleaning up the breakfast mess, they get ready for lunch that begins about eleven. They serve dinner around five in the evening. Any other time is spent on-call in case someone has a sudden hunger attack. Most cooks go to bed about eight at night to get ready for the next day. Many tow companies offer classes so the cooks can keep up-to-date on good nutrition and learn how to prepare these nutritious foods in the most delicious ways. Deckhands and pilots get gourmet treatment on the water.

To balance out these sumptuous meals, many boats have TV rooms with satellite hook-up, video libraries, book and magazine selections, and a well-equipped workout room with all the Nautilus equipment you would find in the bankside gyms. I commented about the good care these people are given. The reason, I was told, is to compensate some for the lives they live on the boats. This led again to the many stories I have heard about the turmoil in their lives, the broken families and all. This time the stories were from a woman, too, Patsy the grocery clerk. She wondered if it was all worth it. She had compassion for them, but kept her distance. After all, it was their choice to do what they do. Though as I have mentioned, some are opting for lesser jobs to get out of it all.

And last, but certainly not least, Ergon was also a pit stop for midstream fueling. Fuel consumption is gauged by horsepower—one gallon per day per horsepower, meaning a twenty-four-hour day. Most of the boats try to go four hundred miles between fueling and they can range from three thousand to twelve thousand horsepower. That's three thousand to twelve thousand gallons of fuel a day at seventy cents or so per gallon and no double stamps on Tuesdays!

After being awed by the magnitude and quality of this riverside store, or should I say warehouse, I went back to my boat ready to continue my journey. The past two days on the river had been relatively easy with no real rough water or bad weather. I looked forward to more of the same.

3. *The Propeller*

From Vicksburg, I headed to Natchez, Mississippi. The water was calm and the scenery repetitious. The river was wide and deep there, but the weather was good, so it was relatively easy going. I pushed on, cautiously riding the waves from passing tows and motivated by the uncertainty of where I would find my next can of gas or where I would find a place to stay for the night out of the weather. Just beyond the levees, though, I could see treetops and tops of what looked like farm buildings and poles with lights on them. I wondered what they looked like. Curiosity was getting the best of me, and I started looking for a place to stop. The banks did not look bad from out in the river. They appeared to be covered with long grass, maybe brome– or Sudan grass, so I went over to have a look.

What looked so neat and well-groomed from the middle of the river, turned out to be grass taller than my head and quite sharp. The bank was not just Mississippi mud, but ragged rocks to hold the mud there. It was more than I was willing to contend with, so I stayed on the river. Conditions like these made this leg of the journey a different kind of trip, with a different character. Even the river water had a gritty feeling to it when I scooped it up and rubbed my fingers through it.

About five miles from Natchez, the motor buzzed like tires spinning on ice as they lose traction. I lost power. But I throttled back and recovered. I had hit something below the surface and broke the rubber hub loose. The last few miles would be easy miles though. I still had some power left and the river current pushed me along. It started to drizzle, so I thought I would take it easy and wait until I got to Natchez where I could fix it in comfort at a dock.

▼

Steve's was another Hoppie's. It was a working man's marina with a couple of old, small barges tied end to end with a shanty for storage, a table for fish cleaning, and remnants of abandoned fuel-handling equipment. The fuel equipment was the casualty of too stringent federal regulations or very vague legal liabilities that the marina was not willing to meet anymore. There was no fuel dockside. I had to hike just over the hill into Natchez for gas. That annoyed the regular customers, but they understood about the overbearing federal regulations. Steve Stevens, the marina owner, was accommodating. He told me where to get gas and helped me tie up around back for protection. The dock was in an area called Under The Hill, about seventy feet below the level of the street where riverside businesses were located.

It was a picturesque place to land. At the top of the long wooden steps on the other side of the road was the Under The Hill Saloon. Out front was a wide-board sidewalk sheltered by a wide verandah with accommodating wooden benches and broad-seated, high, tip-'em-back rocking chairs. The saloon's windows and doors were open without screens giving it an open, airy feel. Guys with brews in hand tipped back in the rocking chairs and yarned stories of their youth to buddies squatting on the edge of the wooden sidewalk. Customers inside were talking through the open windows and doors, either disputing the recollections or egging the yarn spinners on to taller tales, while the bartender carefully saw that no one ran out of "gas." Looking out across the road, those guys had a view of the river that was right off an artist's canvas, surely inspiring them to more creative stories.

A friendly, mannered man a little older than me came forward and inquired, "Where you come from, you old river rat? Now don't deny it, I can tell; you all give yourselves away. You have that look about you. Come on in. What can I do for you?"

Just then, the rain started coming down hard.

"Well, for starters, you have given me some shelter. Now I need a boat dealer close by where I can get a new prop for that Johnson motor," I said.

"Well, there is one across the river in Vidalia, six or seven miles away. It's not close, but if you give me a minute, I'll give him a call to see if he has one and we'll go get it. Where are you going to stay tonight? This rain is going to keep up, and it would be awful wet on that boat of yours. There is a balloon festival here this weekend and most of the places are full, but I'll check with my son and see if we have a room."

He disappeared into his office. He had an inn above and around the saloon, a kind of bed and breakfast called Mark Twain's Inn. That was my introduction to André C. Farish, a Welsh man first and an old-line Southerner second, or was it the other way around? No matter. André had more cubbyholes in his life than a printer's font cabinet. He was intelligent, dashing, had impeccable taste, and was never at a loss for words. André was a host with one hand always occupied, but his eyes were always on you. If there were a hundred guests around him, not one would feel neglected.

He came out of his office with a big smile on his face, assuring me I was welcome to stay. And since I was a river rat, he, of course, gave me the commercial rate for the room. It was done. I would be there until the weather settled down.

Going to get the prop was just a part of the afternoon. André drove an older luxury car that could hold six grown men and still have room for a dog. It was a car built in the days when they had a steel frame to hold them together and had rear-wheel drive. As he drove, he waved at people in passing cars and standing on street corners, and they all waved back. He knew everyone at the boat shop, too. Boats were a subject he knew well.

"Say, I have a boat I'd like to show you," he said. "It's over at my house."

His house was very modest on the outside in a modest neighborhood. The inside was something different. It was elegant, with a touch of French decor and some very classic French antiques as accents.

He showed me his favorite boat, a Boston whaler, that had taken him many a mile—even to Mexico. Seeing he was an experienced sailor, I brought up my question about my fork in the road coming up soon at Baton Rouge: Do I ride the Mississippi River to the very end, or do I avoid the big ships and their associated dangers by taking an alternate route through the Intracoastal Waterway? André's comments were reassuring. He said that if I had come this far in that small boat there were few dangers left that I couldn't handle.

"It's those others who have no spirit of adventure who are keeping you away. It is safe for those who give the river and the big boats their due respect. You would do fine. Come here," he said.

He led me to his office in his house, took out some river charts and went over them with me, giving me more accurate mileage. He noted things to expect, gave me people to contact, and above all, he gave me confidence.

"It's worth going to see, and you can do it, no worries. Go for it, son!"

We spent the rest of the afternoon at a workshop a mile or so away, listening to the rain come down in tankers. Later, back at the saloon, he gave me the key to my room and a tour of the other rooms. They were plush with period furnishings. They had been tastefully decorated and all the stops had been pulled to assure a sense of Southern comfort. The bath, down the hall, of course, was fully carpeted, with live green plants, and full-size bath towels that were plush, thick, luxurious, and folded in one of those old bookshelves with the lift-and-slide glass doors. There was a washer and dryer with no coin slots, brass light fixtures, and a marble-topped commode. The rooms were no less furnished, though some were small. Nothing was spared. It was not what you would expect to find in anything but a fine hotel, let alone an inn tacked onto a saloon.

4. Fish Stories

The rain kept up. It was best, I thought, to get wet and go down to put the top up on the boat to keep some of the water out. It had already rained over three inches in about as many hours with no end in sight. While starting the bilge pump and putting up the top, from out of the haze on the river came a man in his big flat-bottom fishing boat. He pulled up beside me. He was a commercial fisherman, who happened to be the son of Steve, the marina owner. His boat was a real beater—well-used, patched from hard use. He looked at my boat.

"Nice, but a little light. Good for a lake boat but a little light for out here," he said.

And he was right, as I remembered the experience above Hickman. The transom on his boat was a full inch and three-quarters thick to avoid what had happened to me. After our conversation, I enjoyed some real southern barbecue at a place on the corner at Steve's suggestion. Then, I went to my room where sleep was slow to come. Below me in the bar, someone was playing a mean ragtime piano.

▼

The next morning, I went to see how much water had gathered in the bottom of the boat. As I headed down the steps, the sound of a big outboard motor came through the mist to meet my ears. Soon, out of that mist came a johnboat, or as they are known locally a bateau. It was heavily laden with fish. Hanging onto the motor was a man clad in a yellow slicker and oilers. He had thin gray hair and sparkling blue eyes. With practiced skill, he headed his boat to the shore, cut the power, slid gently up on the bank and just before the boat lost all momentum, he gave it full throttle to pin it firmly on the bank. Then, as if in one continuous motion, he lifted the engine and moved forward over his catch, grabbed up the fish and headed over the bow toward the steps which led to his truck on the hill.

After a brief introduction, we hit it off and got right to it. Henry Fitt had been on the river all his life. He was born on it, fished it for his existence, and never thought of ever leaving it. Let me digress for a moment and explain this "born on the river" bit. When he said that, he meant it literally. He lived, and was born, in what we would call a houseboat, what they would call a shantyboat.

The fish Henry was unloading from his boat with little ceremony were the kinds that sport fishermen would talk about for weeks or years afterward. To him, they were the means for paying the bills next month. He pulled a couple of tubs of drum and buffalo, some smallish cats of four to five pounds, and from the bottom of his boat, the last fish he pulled out was a catfish that had its tail on the ground and its open mouth just below his shirt pockets. He estimated forty pounds of fish; a good haul for the day. But he would be disappointed if the next day were not the same. This was a business like any other, and he had expenses to cover.

At wholesale, his fish were worth sixty cents a pound for catfish and twenty-five cents a pound for drum and buffalo. At retail, they sold for a dollar eighty-nine and forty cents a pound, respectively.

All the time he was talking, he was moving around, if not loading his fish, then expressing himself with slow-moving hands or darting clear-blue eyes. After he had loaded his fish, he had to get them to market if he was going to get the best prices. He did not leave briskly, just matter-of-factly, with a smile and a firm handshake with his weathered, callused, but sensitive hands.

5. Plywood Shacks

The next day, it was time for what had become a daily ritual of pumping the water out of the boat. I had tied up behind Steve's crowded dock next to a sterile-looking sort of overgrown aluminum bateau with an aluminum and glass house stuck on top of the whole thing. It looked more like something discarded from a county hospital that had spent too many sessions in its autoclave than the boat it was intended to be.

Several times I had seen a tallish man who was somewhat older than me and drove an older model Lincoln, talking to André. I had never thought of connecting the aluminum boat to him. There seemed to be too much difference between the boat and the man. The man in the Lincoln appeared to be a man of wealth, or at least a man whose wants were comfortably met. As I was working at getting the water out of my boat, there was a rattle of footsteps on that floating aluminum behind me.

"Hi! How ya do-un' this mornun'?"

The words rang out, bouncing off the metal. Glancing around, I first saw a pair of cheap molded-in-one-piece, brown plastic boots. When I looked up to see who was in those boots, there was the Lincoln man carrying two large cans of gas heading for the back of that aluminum thing.

He turned out to be Howard Pritchard Jr., an old-time resident of Natchez. With a little more study, his rumpled pants and Salvation Army "Op Shop" knit shirt did not thoroughly detract from his long, thin fingers, with manicured clean fingernails and his gracious voice. Was he an old river rat of means or was he a man of means who still had river rat in him? It turned out it was a little of both. The acquaintance began there and the cement was laid down by his need to move a boat to a boat ramp with no one around but me and my willingness to help. I took it downriver for him to the landing where he would put it on a trailer for its trip home for the winter.

It seemed whatever his background, he was a Southern gentleman who hung out with his old mates of the river some days and his country club friends on others. And as I was to find out in this land of oil leases and other unexpected wealth, sometimes they were the same people. He told me of the old days of shantyboat people and their shantyboats, the old bateaus and the standby of the day, the putt-putt engines that powered them. Howard said he imagined I'd never seen one of those engines and said he still had one or two out at his place.

"Come on," he said. "I'll show you the ones that have been part of my life."

His house was a few miles out, up a long drive on a gentle slope. Among Southern oaks and pines was a Southern ante-bellum adaptation with a two-story verandah encircling three sides. In the backyard, screened away, except for a privileged few, were the signs of his roots, old boats of his youth. There was the pirogue, a sort of flat-bottom, open-top, double-ended kayak. Howard had some fame for building pirogues around here. There was his old houseboat from the days when his young family was growing. In the barns were more of the beginnings, the motors of the old days, tools, tractors, and other memorabilia. Howard was now one of the few who still knew the significance of it all. As he showed me around the area, we walked past a little building not more than ten-by-twelve feet, made of rough boards and plywood with one window and a screen door.

"Here," he said, "is my getaway."

Inside was a bed, a table and chair, an icebox, an old black-and-white TV, and a hot plate. Hanging through the wall was a small air conditioner. All this was not more than a couple hundred feet from the big house. This shack was a refuge for Howard, a place where he could go to remember who he was and where he came from. It reminded me of others. Thomas Edison, at his laboratory and home in Florida, had his gazebo at the end of a long pier where he went to think. Albert Einstein had his fiddle. The shack, the gazebo, and the fiddle are all a means of getaway, a way to sort out life, to work out the seemingly unsolvable problems at hand. We all need the solitude of a special hideaway for protection from this insane world. Those of us who don't have this can truly go crazy and those of us who do still go crazy at times!

"Was the river my plywood shack?" I wondered.

As we got ready to leave, I asked him about taking a picture of his house.

"Sure, go ahead—hey, let's go have a look at it."

While the house was new, it was full of history, and so was Howard. The furniture was from his ancestors, who looked out from their gilded, framed portraits on the walls, still the overseers of it all. Howard knew some of their histories: the steamboat captains, the business failures, the suicides. Though the house looked old, it had some modern touches. Howard had put concrete and steel in the verandah construction to thwart termites and installed an elevator for his handicapped daughter. Howard also told some of the history of his friends. Steve Stevens, the marina owner, was a man like Howard who could not give up his roots. Oil had made it possible for him to live the good life, which he attempted on the other side of the river. He soon gave up, however, keeping the big house to go to on special occasions, but moving back to where he came from, a mobile home blocked high on the bank where he went out every morning in that old beat-up bateau to check on his oil wells. But now with gum boots on his feet and a seed corn cap perched jauntily on his graying head he carried with him, as did others, one of those fold-up cellular phones in the name of safety, tucked in his coveralls pocket.

Howard remembered he had a business appointment and invited me to tag along. It turned out he had little businesses all around town. As a developer, he knew most people, and they knew him. I mentioned to him I was still looking for a cotton long-sleeved shirt with pockets.

"No problem, my secretary's father has a store that sells such things," he said. Sure enough, I got one from his secretary's father.

"Say, we need to go meet one of my buddies of the river who may have an old-style bateau with one of the old putt-putts in it. He restores them, you know."

Bill Smith, the old shantyboatman, was out for a walk with his dog when we got there, but his daughter and son were there. Both were born on a shantyboat. Their shantyboat was built on a base that looked like a modern mortar box in the range of twelve by forty-two feet with a kind of fishing cabin on top. It had a picket fence around the edge for protection from falling off and to give it a homey appearance. They would live in one place for a while and then move on. A simple and inexpensive way for them to live in those Spartan days. Those days were long gone, she was forty-two and he was forty-seven, and the shantyboat no longer existed.

On the way back, Howard and I talked about cotton and of the damage some were seeing from aerial spraying. Sure, it was helping them make more money but at the expense of the bullfrogs and other natural things. Many were quite upset at what they were seeing, or more accurately at what they were not seeing, as the years passed with continual spraying. And the Corps of Engineers, in their zeal to improve the river, had turned it into a concrete-lined ditch. They had removed the oxbows and other flooded areas, the swamps had dried up, there were not the same numbers of migrating birds, and many of the other animals that were common when Howard was growing up were gone. The way of life that Howard and others had known was disappearing. Even tourists, like me, had become a rarity on the river, he said.

After a long day with Howard, I was ready to get back to my room. It would be the last night at the Under the Hill Saloon and Mark Twain's Inn. The next day would be one of those longish days of more than a hundred miles to the next fuel stop at Baton Rouge. I was lulled to sleep again by the playing of that rinky-tink piano down below. Later, I was to learn André was playing as his way to unwind from the day. Perhaps the piano was André's plywood shack.

6. Merle

The next morning I woke at dawn to a damp fog. As I waited to depart, André came around with his boat. He was a member of the safety crew patrolling the river for the balloon festival he told me about earlier. Soon, it was time to go. The fog had lifted, although the mist was heavy in the sky. About an hour after I left, a call came over the radio.

"*Dulcinea, Dulcinea*, do you copy? This is André. Do you see the balloons?"

"No, it's too hazy here," I replied.

"Just thought I'd check. There are twenty or so up just over the river. Very impressive. Have a good, safe trip and keep in touch. You'll do fine, son!"

Those were things that felt good at times like that.

▼

The river was getting wider and deeper. Most of the time the depth gauge was reading close to a hundred feet for long stretches, not the sixty to eighty feet it had been reading. The width was a consistent mile most of the time. About noon, it was truly warm on the river for the first time in a long time. The thermometer on my jacket said eighty degrees. I took my coat off to feel the sun penetrate deep into my bones. While going along, I saw something ahead in the river. It looked like a log, a yellow log. What was floating down the river now?

The yellow thing was a kayak paddled by Merle, a nice-looking man in his late thirties peeking out from under an Amish straw hat and rainbow sunglasses. We talked for about twenty minutes out there in the middle of the Mississippi River holding on to each other's boats pinwheeling down in lazy circles, enjoying the sun and a chance meeting. For knowledge of the river, he was a wealth of information. He seemed to know all the little side things that were not in the books. He was very close to the subject. Merle had come down the river many times, he said, working on towboats. But that's about all he would say about his personal history.

He had never had a picture of himself in his boat, so I took one. But then, there was no place to send it to him, at least not one that he would admit to. Was he one of those I had heard of? Someone on the river running from or running to something? What were they doing out here all by themselves? We finally said farewell and parted, with a "Maybe I'll see you later," since we both were headed for the same destination.

7. Choice

On the skyline around the bend, haze hung over some sort of industrial complex of huge proportions. It turned out to be a Crown Zellerbach plant for paper products. It covered a large section of land, and on a calm day its odor must have covered the entire county (or since this was Louisiana, the parish). The rest of the way to Baton Rouge was uneventful, with the exception of meeting a couple of the ocean ships I was told to expect the rest of the way down. At least for now, they seemed harmless enough, just big.

The river was tranquil, as was the scenery. But the closer I got to Baton Rouge the more I had to consider the direction of the next part of the trip. Would it be down the Mississippi? Or as had been suggested, the bayou country to the west? If I went down the Mississippi to the zero marker below Pilottown, my Quimby's guide would be of little help. Quimby's Cruising Guide, a manual for river rats, told about places along the river for travelers like me. Even Quimby's discouraged travel on the river beyond Baton Rouge and gave little information, except for some places in New Orleans. I did have some guidance though, from André back in Natchez. I had notes from his charts showing the route to the end of the river, and he had given me people to contact and told me of things to expect. Most of all, he had confidence I could do it.

On the other hand, I did have detailed charts of the Intracoastal Waterway that Bob Jorgenson gave me back in Memphis. This turn-off toward bayou country was coming up at the Port Allen Lock in Baton Rouge. Bob encouraged me to take it, saying it would be a lot more scenic and a lot safer. Others insisted that taking the river down here would be risky and crazy. Some said that if I somehow managed to make it to Pilottown in one piece, coming back upriver to New Orleans or Baton Rouge would be next to impossible. My little boat and motor wouldn't be able to fight the strong downstream current there.

A key landmark, the Huey Long bridge, was coming up. Long was a notorious Robin Hood Louisiana governor and U.S. senator back in the 1920s and 1930s. Long, however, not only allegedly robbed from the rich to give to the poor, he also gave generously to himself for his trouble, or so it is said. One of the things he did for the poor working man was to build a bridge to cross the river and also to protect jobs. Ocean ships were carrying freight farther and farther upstream. They could have gone clear to Natchez, and I was told, in some cases, all the way to Vicksburg. That bypassed the need for the towboats and their barges and all the work of transferring the loads. To protect those jobs, Long built his bridge so low that ocean ships could not get under it. There are smaller ships today that can and do go under the bridge, but the big ships still stop at Baton Rouge, and the tows take it from there.

It was time to decide. Intracoastal Waterway or the Mississippi? Cajun villages or Pilottown? Calm bayous or turbulent, unpredictable river? Scenic, peaceful back-country channel, or raucous, bustling sea-lane? Safety or danger? At the last minute I decided to go for it, to keep going down the river to the end. Where was the spirit of adventure in taking calm, scenic waterways instead of the river? Others had made it, and I could make it too.

PART IV
LOUISIANA

1. *Life Is Fleeting*

The stop for the day was a fleeting operation called Cargo Carriers on the right descending bank, just under the Interstate 10 bridge and past the Port Allen Lock to the Intracoastal Waterway. I had called ahead to make arrangements to stay and to get gas, so they were expecting me. I tied up behind a barge to the side of the retired boat Warren Elsey, which served as the office. Dispatchers Mel and Andy were my hosts for the night.

Fleeting operations like Cargo Carriers are the equivalent of a railroad switchyard. Barges are dropped off and stored or picked up and added to a tow. Along the river in designated locations, these barges are tied to the bank or tied in rows to sea anchors along the edge of the river. When tows come along, they tell the fleeting company what barges need to be added or taken out and a pushboat does the work. With today's technology and increasing demand for efficiency, the tows are usually not put together in a helter-skelter fashion. They are designed more often by a computer model, determining their loads and where they are going.

John Wilder, the vice president of Cargo Carriers, had a soft spot for real river rats. He was a great help in laying out the rest of my trip by advising me where to get fuel and suggesting places to stay that weren't publicized. The next night was taken care of with a simple telephone call to Burnside, Louisiana. It was just a case of who knows who and how they perceive you. I was lucky.

The next morning, there was a heavy, penetrating fog on the river. There would not be an early start today, so I took my time while the fog lifted. While I was getting my stuff together, Merle, in his yellow kayak went gliding by in the mist. As I watched, someone yelled, "Want some fresh nuts?"

My breakfast that day was supplemented with fresh pecans from trees not a hundred feet from where I stood, and I acquired a new skill, cracking pecans by hand. Before then, I had always needed a hammer or nutcracker and a pick. These people didn't have such luxuries, just their hands. It was really simple when someone showed you how: Hold two nuts together in the palms of your hands and squeeze just so, then flick the shells away and eat.

Soon, the fog had lifted enough for me to go. Mel and John had laid out a plan for me to go to Weber's about seventy miles downriver. The next day I'd go another seventy miles into New Orleans, where I'd go through the industrial lock to a canal that led to Lake Pontchartrain, where I'd keep *Dulcinea* for a few days. Mel, John, and others had warned me not to get into New Orleans much past noon. Any time after that and I was likely to get caught at the lock for several hours and then get stuck on the river at night. That was not a good thing to do because of the heavy wakes from big tows and ships. It was also not safe to be alone on a small boat in a big city at night.

About two miles downriver, I met Merle again. He was floundering around in the river in a bend where a heavy blanket of fog was trapped. He seemed blinded and confused in the shroud of mist. Merle was so low he got lost in the fog. My boat was only two feet higher, but it was enough to let me see about a quarter-mile through the fog. Where Merle sat, he could not see much more than the bow of his boat. He did not know there was a towboat coming up the shoot right toward him. He could not even hear it.

"Hey, guy!" I yelled. "You better get out of there or take a big drink, whether you want to or not!"

"Where?" Merle asked.

"Right in front of you, not more than a quarter of a mile. Get going! Now!"

He pushed his paddle in and got out of that situation intact this time. We both went over by the bank and talked some more until the fog lifted a half hour or so later. He was a nice guy, but something kept him very distant. Before leaving him, I saw to it he had a gallon of Gatorade and some suntan lotion, both of which he looked as if he was short on. He did not object to my offerings. He even seemed a little grateful in his way. You wonder about people like him and what's going on behind those eyes.

2. Health Hazard

Below Baton Rouge, there was little to see in the way of nature on the river. There were birds and an occasional animal, but mostly what I saw was manmade. The levees contained the river and in the process changed everything. The view from the river was the levee and what few scrub trees had come up over the years. Sometimes the levees were quite a ways from the river, a quarter of a mile to a mile, with pasture grass and trees of little concern in between.

The river was very gritty and brown. If you ran your fingers through it and put them to your nose, it did not smell like water. Instead, the smell resembled a diluted chemical or slime from a scrub bucket you mopped the kitchen floor with, complete with rainbow colors. The air was worse, too. It cut at my eyes and felt like sandpaper as it went down my throat. But what should you expect with all the chemical plants along the river. To the locals, the stretch of river from Baton Rouge to Burnside-Convent was known as Cancer Alley.

Signs of man were everywhere. There were facilities for the ships and barges where grain, oil, chemicals, fertilizer, and coal were loaded. Over the levees were the plants that produced the goods. These plants lined the river and, as usual, there were few signs to identify them, though on the charts, they were all there—BASF, Shell, and the petroleum companies.

Other signs of man were visible over the levees, such as the rooftops, light poles lining roads, a few radio towers, and the lights that outlined the high school athletic fields. Just north of White

Castle, a roof line suggesting more than a little affluence peeked over the levee. It must have been the home of one of the cotton barons of ante-bellum times. A little after lunch, I saw a rooftop at Plaquemine that I identified as the courthouse. A short time later, on the east bank, peeking over the levees were the tops of the snow-white buildings and the American flag. This was referred to on the charts as a U.S. public health facility for the treatment of Hansen's disease, or leprosy. Built in 1850 near Carville, it's the only one in the continental United States.

The ocean ships had not been the problem or even the danger they were portrayed to be, at least so far. The waves off the bows were large, four to five feet, and I was not told about the crest of those waves, which are from fifty to a hundred feet apart. They weren't turbulent; it was just a big roller coaster ride. That was not near as bad as meeting one of those government launches or a big "Tupperware" cruiser. Those things had vicious wakes that were not too high, just three feet at the most, but very close together and steep-sided. You can get into some serious trouble if you don't hit those waves right. Those were the ones to watch out for, not the ocean ships' waves.

Toward mid-afternoon, the characteristic sight of barges tied up to the banks indicated I was approaching the fleeting area of Weber Marine Services at Burnside. Their office was an old quarter-boat of the Corps of Engineers, which was originally used to house up to thirty-five crew members. It was here that I got a good lesson about this stuff they call revetments that the Corps of Engineers put down to stabilize the banks from erosion damage. Here the material was crushed stone the size of a basketball, though the stones were anything but round and smooth. They resembled tiger's teeth that were ready to eat anything that got near. I saw it along the bank and selected what seemed to be an innocent-looking spot to nudge up on. What I did not see was what was down under the water.

The prop went tick, tick, tick. I had run into something I could not see, so I tried to back out. Again, but louder, the prop went TICK, TICK, TICK! I had gotten stuck like a fish hook, and it was going to be harder getting out. Something under there was trapping me. After trying to gently find a way out to little avail, I tipped the motor up. Those ticking sounds did not sound that bad, but the prop looked like it had lace tatted around its edges. After poking around for what seemed like an eternity, I almost gave up hope. But then, the boat just floated free. I didn't realize someone was watching my struggle until I heard the deadpan voice coming from the quarterboat barge.

"Why don't you go around to the south end and tie up on the inside. Then come on back and we'll see about getting you some gas."

I crossed over the levee to get some gas at the Burnside general store. If a Northerner were to imagine a poor, black, Southern town, Burnside would fit his stereotypical notions. The best two buildings I saw were the pure white combination general store/Texaco station and the church. Between carts of gas, I bought a couple pieces of fried chicken that were sold from a glass box by the checkout. It was fried to perfection, the kind gourmet cooks write about and wish they really knew how to cook. I took my chicken to a swing under the porch on the front of the quarterboat where I watched the river while I ate. How easy it was to be satisfied as time went on; it was the little things.

People in Burnside sat on porches doing family mending and passing gossip. Most townspeople worked in riverside chemical factories and refineries doing dangerous jobs for inadequate wages. They lived in the shadows of these plants, breathing polluted air. I realized our country enjoys cheap gas and bargain synthetic fabric at their expense. It reminded me of stories from the Old South of sharecropping and slavery. Back then, sharecroppers were at the mercy of the landowners with little chance to earn their way out, and slaves did dirty, dangerous work with no way out. This was, of course, very economical for consumers, but unfair to the workers. This unfairness was in present-day Burnside, too, where the workers lived in the dust and waste of the factories, with little or no chance for escape. Unlike plantation owners and overseers of long ago, the factory owners and CEOs don't live near the workers. They are isolated from the squalor in their townhouses or villas with a sea breeze and a mountain view. They don't have to look these workers in the eye; they can't empathize with them. If they saw this, surely they would change their ways, wouldn't they?

▼

Later, I talked to Wayne La June, the night dispatcher at Webers. He was a Cajun boat captain who came from a long line of rivermen. He started in high school part-time, then finally worked his way up to lineboat captain, making $200 a day. Then, as others I met, he found all that glittered was not gold and gave it up for a job where he was home every night. He told me how they used to catch freshwater shrimp in 1965 right out there, pointing through the window, not anymore. According to him, no one should eat the fish from the river.

"Too many chemical plants...don't care what they say about their concern for waste disposal. We see the fish, they're not fit to eat, not by us, anyway. It's not all our waste, either. You know it all starts up North and multiplies as it works down. Then we just put the icing on the cake, so to speak."

The rest of the night the conversation was not of trivial things, not of business, or sports, or girls. It was of life—life on the river, life up North. He was as curious about me as I was about him. The tough riverman seemed to have a sensitive side that came out if he felt safe. He exhibited a caring for his family that was contrary to the fact that his life could be so tumultuous. This sensitivity seemed to be true of most rivermen I met. In the last glimmer of light, I looked out the window as Merle went by in his yellow kayak. Where would he be tonight? I wondered.

After hours of talking, I decided to call it a night. I went down to my boat and made my bed under the canopy in the bottom. I lay there rocking to the rhythm of the passing boats and thought about the day ahead. New Orleans was just seventy miles down river. It would be the end of the trip for most who came down the river, but not me.

3. Through the Backdoor

The next morning, after the fog burned off, I was back out on the river. I saw a big, pink Norwegian freighter being turned around by tugs. I didn't want to follow it all the way to New Orleans, so I darted out and made haste.

On the river, the air was hazy, humid, polluted, and cut my throat. It was an incentive to make good time. On smooth water, going fast was fun because of the familiar swishing as the boat drove along. Soon, a breeze came up and the tow traffic increased, which churned the water, but my boat was still going at a reasonable pace, or so I thought.

Suddenly, I got a strange feeling at my back. I looked around. It was the Norwegian freighter—all six hundred feet of it— bearing down on me a quarter mile or so back. My motor was whining and roaring, and my fourteen hundred pound boat was skimming and bouncing along while this 100,000-ton ship was gliding easily, silently creeping up on me. The freighter pushed a six-foot bow wave ahead of it and discharged slow impulses of engine exhaust from the stacks on the top of its ten-story building. There was no sound. It was humbling!

The freighter passed me, and I followed it for about ten miles, then the ship was gone. It was pleasant following something so big. It literally smoothed the waters. The boat not only blocked the wind but blocked the traffic—no one bluffs with something that size.

▼

Fisherman Henry Fitt of Natchez, Mississippi, lugs a hefty catfish up from the river toward his pickup.

The Under the Hill Saloon and Mark Twain's Inn in Natchez, Mississippi

I'm fixing my propeller at Steve's Marina.

I'm docking Dulcinea *at a marina off the river in New Orleans on Lake Pontchartrain.*

When bar pilots board ocean ships near the mouth of the Mississippi River, the ship doesn't stop; the pilots must board while the ship is moving by climbing from a smaller pilotboat and scaling the side of the larger ship on a rope ladder.

Chief engineer George Spiridonos (right) and a crewmate (left) stand before a wall of dials, guages, levers, and knobs that control and monitor their Greek ship traveling through Southwest Pass on its way to the Gulf of Mexico.

Concrete walkways are the sole means of transportation over the marshy ground of Pilottown, Louisiana. The large white building at right is the pilot compound.

At Delta Marina in Empire, Louisiana, Fish carries on with business as usual—even on Halloween.

Near Houma, Louisiana, you need to look for more than fellow boatmen on the bayou. Pontoon planes are a common sight, suddenly appearing from the sky and touching down on the water.

Bobby Boudreaux's boatyard on the bayou in Lafitte, Louisiana, wasn't much to look at, but his crew builds skiffs that are works of art.

Dulcinea was hoisted onto a trailer at McKinney Towing in Baton Rouge, Louisiana, at the end of her voyage.

Traffic on the river was changing. There were fewer boats like mine on the river. I was the intruder in this part of the blue collar river. The closer New Orleans got, the more I saw ocean tugboats and barge traffic. In the sky were signs of the big city—buzzing busyness of airplanes flying overhead. In the city, activity along the bank was continuous. Tankers, container ships, and grain haulers being loaded and unloaded. There was steady motion all along both sides of the river. There was no relief, even on a Sunday morning.

Entering a city from the river is different than by road. By road, it is like coming to the front door of a house. You go from the rural settings to the mowed lawns up neatly trimmed sidewalks, sometimes past lovingly tended flower gardens to attractive front entrances, then into front halls or living rooms where you are made welcome. Coming to a city by river is like coming up a back alley, past a vegetable garden, around the corner of the garage, stepping by garbage cans, ducking under clotheslines, and arriving at the back door, where there are muddy boots and leaf rakes or snow shovels awaiting future use. Inside the backdoor, one set of steps leads to the basement and the other to the kitchen, where the smell of food being prepared greets you as you move to the living room. You are going to the same place in the end, there are just different ways to get there; the paths give the same results with a different perspective. (There are exceptions on the river to this backdoor rule, such as Memphis and Vicksburg in the south and Fort Madison and Davenport in Iowa which give their face to the river. But they are the exceptions.)

▼

From the first time I saw signs of New Orleans to the time I went under the bridge at the foot of Canal Street was about ninety minutes (from noon to half past one). I was ecstatic about achieving this major milestone of the trip. In childlike abandon I pulled out my cellular phone, and in the middle of the river, I called a select few loved ones back home to share my joy as the New Orleans river bridge passed over my head.

4. Crescent City Mooning

New Orleans was a resting place for me. I wanted to clean up and reorganize, as well as spend some time with an old friend, Tom Halverson, and his wife, Judy. They used to live in Des Moines, in a historic district called Sherman Hill. They had a period home there that they had restored, and when they came to New Orleans, they moved into another period home with plans to bring the Southern house to its previous grandeur. They lived on Urania Street, just a little off Saint Charles, a couple of miles from the French Quarter and a half mile from the Garden District.

New Orleans was similar to other river towns I had visited. The local newspaper was abuzz with the hype of casino gambling boats that were slowly trying to make it through the maze of the Southern politics of Louisiana Governor Edwin Edwards, a contemporary version of Huey "Kingfish" Long. It appeared that Edwards' family wanted a piece of the action. They wanted to be an official supplier of necessary items for the casino boats. Local police wanted off-duty jobs as security personnel and threatened to strike if they were not allowed to do that. Some were willing to give up many years of service on the police force for these lucrative side jobs.

New Orleans was an unsettling city for me because of the high level of crime. Those who lived there were acclimated, I guess, though it is not a prospect that had any appeal to me. Everything was locked, there were bars on steering wheels and nothing showing in cars when people left them. There were constant warnings:

"Be cautious of that street. Don't walk on that side of the street. Stay out of that neighborhood at night." The postal offices had armed police. A grocery store I went to had armed guards in the parking lot and a tower by the street with a guard in it who could close the gates to keep a perpetrator from leaving. Homes had iron fences around them that were locked; the car inside the fence was parked and locked; the house was locked; the whole mess was protected with alarm systems. These places were not just locked, as normal people would lock them. They had locks like the courthouse gate in Vicksburg, with chains and padlocks. Even a local bank had a masonry wall around it and iron gates with anchor-sized padlocks and chains. No one could justify the size of these locks unless they expected to be attacked with a vengeance.

It was too much for this small-town kid. I wondered if this chain-and-padlock mentality could be a cultural difference going back to the early days of the Spanish and French? I don't recall seeing this tradition in the New England states where the Anglo-Saxon was the major player in developing culture.

Tom ran an antique store in an area you would not normally have expected to find antiques and other high-priced things. The part of town had elegance, but it also had the seamier part of society there with it. A few doors away from Tom's store was a hardware store that reflected the area. When I entered the store, I was stopped short by a counter running across the front to bar further intrusion. Behind the counter was an older, well-worn lady in a jacket with generous pockets. Behind her was the store. There were shelves filled with merchandise, but out of reach. You had to know what you wanted and ask for it. There was no shopping or browsing and you did not know what she had, only if she had what you asked for. It was a new twist. The store had bars on the doors, bars on the windows, and to keep the door secure after hours, a chain and padlock.

I spent a day at the marina cleaning stuff up and relocating the bilge pump to get more water out. Then there was some rope to cut away from the prop; the remains of some two-inch rope that had been floating out in the river had gotten tangled up there. It was just another hazard that was part of river travel.

After cleaning up, I spent the next couple of days seeing the sights. Even though New Orleans made me uneasy with its crime and paranoia, it was still a good town with lots of interesting things to experience such as the food, the houses, the history, and the traditions. One morning, Tom and I rode the streetcar to the French Quarter and walked the historic district and ended up at the Café du Monde, a sidewalk cafe, where we indulged ourselves with beignets, a French doughnut with powdered sugar, and ice coffee, laced with chicory and lots of milk. We watched people go by and listened to others talking as they ate their beignets and drank their coffee.

While in New Orleans, I made plans to get on the Intracoastal Waterway through Cajun country after returning from the end of the river. The final leg of the trip would end up at Cargo Carriers across the river from Baton Rouge. I arranged to leave the boat there while I went back north to Des Moines to get the truck and haul my friend *Dulcinea* home. But first, I'd have to get to the end of the river and the powers-that-be were wary of my journey when I tried to make arrangements. I called the New Orleans bar pilots' office and got hold of Captain John Peterson for information about my final stop on the river, Pilottown. Peterson was helpful, but initially he was not encouraging. He gave stern cautions about the river and what to expect. Before closing, he gave his tacit blessing when he gave me the name of a person to contact when I got there. Later, Peterson even said he would contact him so he would know I was coming.

"By the way," he added. "Call me before you leave and tell me a target date for your arrival there."

The conversation I had with the Coast Guard was not that cordial. They were friendly, but would not talk openly till I assured them the tape recorder I had would not be used to record any of the conversation while I was with them. I gave my assurance and took the tape out of it. From then on, it was just a "factual conversation" with their facts. They discouraged me, or anyone who was not engaged in commercial business in a commercial boat, from going below New Orleans on the river. With the boat I had, they were not at all happy about the prospect.

I wondered about all of this. I found their warnings similar to a story of Mark Twain's. When he returned from Europe, he learned a newspaper said he had died, to which he replied, "Reports of my death have been greatly exaggerated." That was how I took much of what I had been told of the big, bad things down there as greatly exaggerated. I was going to eat the elephant one bite at a time, but one element was holding me back—the weather. Every morning it started blowing or raining or both. If the weather had just cooperated, I could have continued. The rain and wind was not enough to stop me if I just had it on the river, but I was five miles away from the river on Lake Pontchartrain and the wind was an obstacle there. The lake was only twenty feet deep and twenty miles across, but with a 10 mph wind across that distance, the waves were not good for such a small boat. I was trapped and if conditions did not change soon, I was tempted to hunt around for someone to haul me to the river, which was just two miles away as the crow flies. It wasn't that the fresh bananas from Tom's trees, with their distinctive lemon flavor, were not nice or smelling the jasmine at night when the nectar flows was not romantic, it was just that I wanted to get back on the river and not be land-bound. I was only two days from Pilottown, and my ultimate goal seemed at last within easy reach. But with the delay, the bad weather pushed my final destination further away.

5. Just Another Day

Finally, after a week in New Orleans, the weather cleared. By ten o'clock, I was back on the river and strangely felt more at home than I had on land. I ended up staying in New Orleans for a week. That was too long in one place.

The trip to Empire was very enjoyable. The weather was warm, shirt-sleeve weather, for one of the few times this trip. I passed about a dozen ships coming down this stretch of the river, three tows, and numerous workboats. It was not a place to space off. I had to be alert, give everyone lots of room, and remember that I was the smallest one on the river. The levees were gone along the banks. It was now delta land with marshes just inches above the water level. But still along the river, there was not much nature, just commerce and industry.

The few towns along here were set back and seemed to have turned their backs to the river, even though their incomes were generally derived from it one way or another. It was unbelievable that they would do this. Thinking on it more, however, I began to understand. People in the mountains don't spend all their time in them; people on lakes are not all devoted fishermen and most farmers are not hobby gardeners. The thing you are around the most retains an enduring fascination for some but for most it begs for distance when the day is done.

There was a canal off the river leading to Empire. To get there, I had to go through a lock. On the other side of the lock I was transported to what could have been a scene from John Steinbeck's

Cannery Row—sinking boats, dilapidated docks, and factories. Then there were signs of regenerating prosperity. The Asians, with their extended families, seemed to be major contributors judging from the names on the boats and the processing facilities.

That night, I stayed at the fuel dock of Delta Marina, a primary supplier for the small fisherman. The marina was also the neighborhood store and bar. They also sold charts and spark plugs. Jimmy, the marina's chief cook and bottle washer, suggested I sleep in my tent over by his big pole shed to keep away from the mosquitoes that would be coming out at sundown. There was to be a chance of some unsettling weather. After dinner I settled down to the relaxing sound of mosquitoes. Jimmy came by on his three-wheeler and asked if I wanted to pack up and stay at his house for the night. "No, this will be fine, but thanks for asking."

Another sound I was to become acquainted with was the sound of the shrimp boats and the oyster dredgers coming in, until about one thirty in the morning. Just two hours later, the same boats were on the way out with the deep rumble of the big engines buried inside them. All in all, it was a comfortable night despite the few distractions.

▼

The next morning started with a beautiful sunrise. The sun sparkled on the heavy dew that covered everything. This was my last day going south. My goal was about to be realized. Helicopter traffic had been heavy since leaving New Orleans and now, as I neared Venice, it increased dramatically as they serviced the oil platforms. Venice was a headquarters and last jumping-off point for servicing the numerous oil platforms in the Gulf. The traffic of the very large crewboats also increased. They left Venice on the west bank, crossed the Mississippi and went into the Gulf on the east side of the river, where the low banks have given way to little more than just tussocks of tall grasses. It was vital to stay alert as the sizes of the ships made it difficult to judge distance and speed.

That morning at a quarter past ten I turned to the last chart, covering the section to the end of the river, including Pilottown. I had gone through two books of charts, and now they had meaning for me, with a story for every page. These pages were not just sterile information anymore. I felt connected with them. Then I saw the waterway leading back to Pilottown!

After passing by the commercial dock where the pilotboats were tied, there was a beautiful little water trail leading back to a tropical setting of white buildings with metal roofs, green vegetation, and elevated sidewalks. This isolated little town appeared as if it was right out of a fairy tale. Around noon I pulled up to the dock. There was not much time for reflective thinking about coming to the end of the journey because the questions started coming almost immediately.

"Where you from?" asked a young man who watched me pull up to the dock.

"Minneapolis, six weeks ago...I think," I said.

"Well, you must be hungry," the man said.

He seemed to infer that I hadn't taken nourishment since I started the trip.

"Let's get something to eat. There's plenty. You have all you want, then let's hear some of it. Here, it's this way."

He led me to the pilot's headquarters in one of the white buildings and to their perpetually ready buffet where there was salad, sausage, biscuits, fruit, lasagna, and much more.

"What you have to drink? We have anything but alcohol. Help yourself!"

Within what seemed to be just microseconds, there were new people in my life: Dave Smith, Leon, T.J. Pazani, Glen, Larry, and Charlie. They were all pilots full of stories, questions, and the phrase, "Have you had something to eat yet, there's plenty!"

Captain Svenson, the chief of this work shift came by.

"Hey," he said. "How you doin'? Had something to eat yet?"

▼

It was still early in the day and the weather was to be unsettling for the next few days. I asked about going down to the zero marker, the official end of the river, and decided to do it right away. Below Pilottown, the Mississippi River forked off in several different directions, looking something like a bird's foot on the map. Each of these passes took a different route to the Gulf of Mexico. The zero marker was set at the beginning of the Southwest Pass, South Pass, and Pass a Loutre (French for "Otter Pass"), an area known as Head of Passes.

There it was. The marker was a nondescript day marker on a steel tower about fifteen feet high, anchored to a pile of rocks. There was no "0" on it, just a blank green diamond. There were no bells, no whistles.

Here I was, at the official ending point of a long journey. I had done it! There was no elation, no letdown—it just seemed to happen. But there was not indifference either. I spent a few minutes here reminiscing over the past weeks with thoughts too deep to sort out and took a couple of pictures. Then I did something I had not done since I started this journey. I pointed *Dulcinea* upriver. I returned to Pilottown. The wind whipped the greenish-gray water and ships passed by with little notice of entering or leaving one of the great rivers of the world. To them, it was just another day.

6. Southwest Pass

Pilottown's chief industry is piloting and its primary purpose is to serve as a sort of way station for specially trained bar pilots and river pilots. Bar pilots take control of ocean ships on the river between Pilottown and the Gulf, while river pilots guide ships between Pilottown and New Orleans. Another group of pilots, called NO-BR pilots, take ships between New Orleans and Baton Rouge.

Bar pilots' specialized training and skill is needed to guide ships through Southwest Pass, a treacherous channel with a tricky current and shallow water. River pilots are specially trained to guide ocean ships above Pilottown through a river channel that's relatively straight, though the current is fast and unpredictable. Bar pilots work shorter hours at a stretch (it takes about two hours to get through Southwest Pass), but their chances for accidents, such as grounding ships, spilling cargo and blocking channels, are greater. River pilots aren't exposed to these risks, but they have to work longer hours at a stretch (about eight hours), and negotiate more traffic, so it all balances out. River pilots have a more aristocratic background. Bar pilots are more well-educated cowboys and able risk-takers. Neither one has a cream-puff job. Their jobs are just different.

Toward evening, the bar pilots gathered in the dayroom to sit and talk. I took special note of one pilot. He was in the background away from the rest of the group, but his presence still commanded attention. He had a patriarchal image about him. He was a graying man in casual clothes that hung on him with an air of dignity. He had kindly eyes that saw all and ears that did not protrude, although they missed not a word. I had seen that he knew his job and got it done, not while you were looking, but in the blink of an eye. He did not stand erect, but he was a tall man in spirit. This was Captain Louie Miller.

As we talked, the pilots expressed more than subtle feelings of hostility toward writers in Pilottown. In the past, the *National Geographic*, as well as other national magazines and newspapers, had sent people down to do stories. From their reactions, I gathered that some of the reporters must have had their own agendas and caused some friction among all concerned. When I mentioned I was writing about my travels, some of the pilots seemed to let it pass or shrugged it off, but others cooled a little. One of those who chilled when I mentioned my writing was Captain Louie Miller, although he didn't say anything.

The thing that bothered these men most was that some writers had portrayed them as men who simply inherited their jobs, like royalty. It's not that simple. And in their ignorance, these reporters even questioned whether pilots were still needed, portraying the noble profession as a make-work job. These smug reporters, who think they've seen and heard it all, came down and wrote how bar pilots get their jobs by having the right connections. These "objective" reporters saw themselves removed from these circumstances in their own jobs. It's true that piloting generally runs in families and that bar and river pilots are members of an exclusive organization. But in what job does having "right connections" not play a part? In my own life, I have had some experiences with this. The carpenter's union in Iowa was officially organized in such a way that you couldn't join the union unless you had a job and you couldn't get a job unless you were a member of the union. So how did I get in? My father wrote insurance policies for a large building contractor. One day Dad called the contractor and said, "Hey, I need a favor." Voilà! Union card. And so it goes. In the white-collar world, how many times does the best job go to the person who knows the right things, compared to the person who knows the right people? It happens in dentistry, law, politics, on the fighting field bucking for chicken colonel, and I would imagine in journalism too.

What those writers failed to mention was that training to become a pilot is long and demanding and that only the best of the best are allowed to become pilots, connections or no connections. For most bar pilots, the training started before they even knew it, since they were born into pilot families. Many times, before they were out of high school, they began working part-time and summers on the river as deckhands. From there, if the interest was great enough, they would work for a third mate's ticket, which takes about three years at sea on ships. Then, they had to go to maritime college and spend another year at sea. Finally, they had to apply for the job of bar pilot where only the best are accepted. If accepted, they had to serve a five-year apprenticeship and accumulate forty round trips to New Orleans, forty round trips through Southwest Pass, and twenty more of any combination. After this, they were again reviewed for final acceptance, and not all make it. The river pilots who take the ships from Pilottown upriver to New Orleans and Baton Rouge have a very similar program. Yes, this is an exclusive club, but the dues are high.

As the evening progressed, some in the group suggested I go on down the Southwest Pass, beyond the zero marker. After all, I had come this far, I might as well go all the way to the Gulf, they said. I could surely handle it in good shape.

"No," I said. I was satisfied with what I'd done, and I didn't share their confidence in me.

"Why not? It's just twenty-four miles."

"No, that's OK."

It was dropped, I thought. Then, about nine o'clock, Charlie, a bar pilot, asked, "Have you ever climbed up the side of a ship?"

"Well, no, but I've never done a lot of things."

"Get your life jacket. I'm leaving in ten minutes. Come with me, OK?"

"Well..."

"No 'well'; just get your stuff and let's go. They won't wait, you know!"

Hurrying along behind Charlie down the darkened dock toward the warmed-up pilotboat, I thought, "What are you getting yourself into this time Knuds? Sometimes you just walk right into some real doozies."

The pilotboat was a thirty-five foot blue-collar Chris Craft, high-powered, reasonably fast, and very seaworthy. Once inside, we headed out to a freighter going downriver to sea with a load of soybean meal. The ship did not stop. We pulled up beside it in the middle of the river. Our pilot pushed hard against the hull, which was protected by a row of airplane tires hung around the sides. We were going about 15 mph when we boarded the ship by climbing up the side on a rope ladder. This climb was not excessively high, about fifteen feet, but high enough for me. I guess it was the excitement of it all, but under normal circumstances, this was not something I would rush out to do. Up the ladder Charlie went with the advice, "Hold on to the sides and don't look down!" The other bit of advice was obvious: "Don't fall!" The landing from the fall would have been against steel at best, and at worst, between two boats or in the water where I would have been sucked into the propeller of the ship.

Up I went, not even thinking about falling. My thoughts were of the adventure of doing something most people just read about and going places I had never dreamed of. Things were going so fast and the darkness blurred all the factors involved, such as the real size of the ship, its condition, and who was at the top to receive us aboard. On deck, we were quickly ushered to the bridge at the top of four long, steep flights of metal stairs into the dimly lit world of the captain and his second officers, all peering into the dark, glancing at the radar, and calmly receiving the bar pilot and me. Thereafter, the ship and its safe passage to the sea was in the hands of this youngish "Captain Charlie," who would use his wisdom and knowledge to guide the ship for the next twenty-four miles of water through the Southwest Pass.

He took control of the ship in a very low-key manner, pleasantly asking for information, such as the draft of the ship (meaning how deep it was in the water), the present speed, and the rpms of the engine. These were all visible on the gauges over the windows, but he checked them out with questions anyway. From this information, Charlie gave orders, no, not orders, but rather soft authoritative requests to the captain, who relayed the information to the officer steering the ship or to the engineer below. As time went on and the initial rush subsided, I learned this was a Greek ship with a Greek crew. Its load was going to Colombia.

Someone asked me, "Would you like some coffee?"

Charlie prompted: "Yes, you want some coffee."

This was Greek coffee, served in a small demitasse cup. It was a kind of instant coffee with one spoon of coffee, one spoon of sugar, and a glass of water in case you swallowed some of the crud that settled at the bottom. It was strong enough to keep you awake for a week.

In the dark Charlie guided this foreign ship down familiar waters with assuredness and calm. He had no headlights, no way to stop on the proverbial dime, and made split-second decisions that could take fifteen or more minutes to undo. As we moved through the night, a different world opened up. I saw why the pilots protected their night vision as musicians protect their hands or a singer his voice. Their vision, along with their knowledge of the river, is a vital part of their job.

Looking out toward both banks from ten stories above the river's surface, the shadowy Gulf was visible over the grass. It was a sight I couldn't see from my usual vantage point on the river. Out there were the lights on the oil platform, little white lights that outlined everything above the water making it look like Christmas. In the channel, where we were, the shoreline was black and the water sparkled, reflecting ship lights, the lighted buoys, and flashing day-markers. On the radar screen Charlie pointed out the loading facilities, small boats, and barges. It was all there if you knew what to look for. On the bridge, it was respectfully quiet. Voices were low and polite, not standoffish or aloof, or even the tone of those wanting their space; just quiet. I wondered if it was quiet because of the intensity of it all. The crew on the bridge had looks on their faces that made me think they were in another world thinking of other places, or even other times.

These guys didn't dress stuffy as you might think from watching *The Love Boat*. They're not sea captains and officers of luxury liners. They're just guys making a living and dressing comfortably doing it. They wore rubber-soled Nikes, causing no tell-tale scuffing as they moved around. From the bridge, the big engines seemed to have sneakers on, too. There was just a low, unobtrusive rumble.

When there seemed to be a lull in the action, Charlie told me of the early days of Mississippi passes. There were three: Southwest (where we were), the South, and Loutre or East Pass. Neither the South nor the Loutre passes had been used commercially since Civil War days. Southwest had been favored since the late 1700s, in the days of the Spanish. There has always been some sort of settlement near the river's mouth that was established for the business of navigating ships into the river. Some were washed out by hurricanes. The current Pilottown was established around 1857.

After Pilottown was established, there were still many problems with navigation and with keeping the channel open. In the late 1800s, a river engineer named James Eads kept the pass open by building jetties. Eads also invented the diving bell, built the first iron bridge across the Mississippi at Saint Louis in 1874, and built armor-plated gunboats that helped the Union secure the river during the Civil War. Eads' jetties were like walls built into the water that narrowed the channel. By narrowing the channel, he increased the speed of water flowing through it, which took more sediment into the Gulf. That prevented sand bar buildup and scoured a deeper, more navigable channel.

Maintaining the deep water necessary for the big ships is still an ongoing project at the mouth of the Mississippi. The forever changing delta at the end of the river is a constant challenge for bar pilots. In the passes, the river varies in depth with the change in water flow and the silting that follows. Contrary to what you would think, the river gets shallow in times of high water. It dumps more silt from upriver flooded areas than it can wash away. As the water goes down, the river dumps less silt and is less clogged with sand and sediment. The Corps of Engineers is constantly doing soundings with a specially equipped boat that records the river depth and prints it out on a graph. The graphs are reviewed by pilots and with this knowledge and their experience, they guide the ships "over the bar," that is through the passes that are prone to silting and the buildup of sandbars.

One pilot told me there are times when a boat will have a thirty-five-foot draft and the river is only thirty-five feet deep, so they have to plow through. In times like that, when scraping the bottom, you can feel it in the ship, hear it in the engines, and sense it in the way the ship responds to the rudder. Those are the times when bar pilots earn their wages.

▼

Out on the flying bridge, I wandered around, looking forward and back and over the sides. Down below, there was a chop on the water that would have caused me some very attentive moments in *Dulcinea*. Up here, though, it was tranquil. The ship slipped along as if detached from it all, with no disturbances. Clouds crossed the midnight sky, covering and then exposing the moon. The scene could play mind games with you—Captain Kirk on the *Enterprise*, floating through space—if you didn't concentrate on your surroundings. Charlie motioned me back inside, and pointed out a situation on radar with two ships two miles ahead that were passing each other, one going on down and the other coming toward us. What he would do now would determine what would happen when we met those ships. Out here, this was close-range navigation and once something was decided, there was no going back. I watched while this happened. We held back to give them space. If we had kept our original pace, there would not have been room, as the three of us would have been at the same place, where there was just barely room for two, at the same time.

Later, while wandering around, I passed a large floor grate behind the bridge. Looking down into it was almost painful. The heat coming up was doing its best to emulate a blast furnace down there. I figured out I was looking right down on top of the engine. There were no fans down there forcing this air up; it was coming up by convection and was strong enough to blow your hat off. What sort of thing was this that could push this boat with such authority, yet seem docile enough to be controlled with the slightest touch, like a rider's knee on the side of a horse?

My thoughts were interrupted by a soft voice.

"Would you like to go down there and see it?"

He introduced himself as Miofas George, saying his names in the reverse order from us. He was the navigator from the Greek island of Chios, the same place the captain, Kalouais Argirij, was from, as were most of the better seamen and shipowners of Greece. I followed him down the flight of stairs we had come up to the deck. Then we went farther down and down and down, from decks to catwalks with steps as steep as ladders. Then, there was the engine, smallish by ocean standards, but sufficient for this ship. It had eight thousand horsepower in what is called a cross-head medium speed—seven cylinders, twenty-one inches in diameter and a sixty-inch stroke with a top speed of 150 rpms. The noise was overwhelming, as was the heat.

The chief engineer, George Spiridonos, stood proudly beside it all, surrounded by pushrods the size of baseball bats and rocker arms that weighed more than an old V-8 car engine. The rhythm of the engine was that from the story of the *Little Engine That Could* as it went joyously over the hill—"I think I can, I think I can, I think I can...I thought I could, I thought I could, I thought I could." From there we walked into a room the size of a row house kitchen, where one wall was covered with dials, gauges, lights, toggle switches, rheostats, levers, and knobs that monitored and controlled it all. There was a machine shop in another area of the ship, where piston rings that looked like barrel hoops hung on the wall. They were capable of doing all but the very major type of repair work. Repairs were not done on board simply for the pride of being able to do it. They had to be able to solve problems in emergencies for the safety of the crew and cargo.

Earmuffs, to protect crew members hearing, were a must in that part of the ship. In the 100-degree-plus heat near the engine, the standard dress for sweaty, shiny-faced workers was short-sleeved shirts (some with alligators on them), short pants to match, and thongs for foot gear. Comfort first was the attitude. Protect your ears and other safety would take care of itself. This might seem careless by our standards, but it was adequate for these self-reliant men of the sea. One of the engine room workers explained to me that if you were going to get burned, it was better to have just the skin burned rather than polyester melted to skin. And if you dropped something on your foot—it was all heavy—it was better for the doctor to get right to it than have to pry a steel-toed shoe away first.

▼

Later, back on the bridge, Charlie motioned to me. It was time to get ready to go. The pilotboat was on its way and we would be boarding soon. Charlie had turned control back over to the captain as the ship prepared to go to sea. We went down the stairs and to the side of the ship. Charlie went over first to show me how.

"Don't look down and hold tight when you get on the boat!"

It was all over before I knew it. We were inside the boat, heading for the station at the end of the Southwest Pass. We would be leaving the station at one in the morning, two hours from now.

7. Sirens of the Sea

What a day. At this time the night before, I had been in Empire sleeping. In the morning, I wondered what the day would bring. At noon I was a stranger in Pilottown, and at eleven that night I was at a way station waiting to go back to Pilottown. I had something to eat, and then found a cozy bunk to get some rest. My mind was reeling from it all.

At half past twelve Charlie knocked on the door; he had a better idea. Instead of going back at one in the morning with him as planned, he thought it would be better to go back up the pass at five with Louie Miller, the aloof yet grandfatherly pilot from the night before.

"Why not go back with him." Charlie said. "You could see the sunrise and a little of the Gulf. So far, you haven't seen much in the dark."

So I went back to sleep, sort of; there was too much going on. At four I was awake and wanted to walk around. I could sleep later. There wasn't far to go. The station was similar to an oil platform high on pilings. Up there was a kitchen, radio room, day room, laundry room, spacious bathroom for cleaning up, and the dormitory rooms. The generator and maintenance shop were out in another building. During the day, there would no doubt be a spectacular view of the Gulf. Time was going so fast. Louie was there in no time.

"Come on, we're going," he said. Down the steps we went, jumped on the pilotboat, and were off toward the dark shadow of the ship in the Gulf.

This one I got straight. It was Dutch-owned, leased to a Belgian company and had a Russian crew. The name on the side said it was the *Kilchem Mediterranean*, a chemical transport carrying 7,350 tons of molasses (about five barge loads) from Colombia to New Orleans, which might either end up in cattle food or in soft oatmeal cookies on the grocer's shelf. As we neared the ship, it was apparent there would be little, if any, climbing to board. It was small and heavy in the water; it looked as if you could just step on, except the waves were five to six feet high out in the Gulf. Timing would have to be good to hop aboard as the two boats bobbed around. It seemed to me a little dangerous. There must have been concern among the others, too. We didn't head straight to the ship like we did the night before on the river. We hung off a hundred feet or so for quite some time. Being unfamiliar with all the goings-on, it was not apparent to me right away that the ship was slowly turning as we followed beside it. But soon the wind was coming over the far side of the ship. We were in its break, and the water calmed. Then our pilotboat came alongside the ship, and we were able to just step on! There was no boat bobbing, no ladders to climb. The ship returned to its normal course as we went to the bridge.

Politics and border changes are so far reaching. This was not a truly Russian crew, I learned. There was only one crew member from Russia aboard. Previously, crew members were all citizens of the Soviet Union. Now, although they were the same men, they were Ukrainian, Latvian, and Georgian, with one Russian. They did not work for the motherland anymore. They were capitalists, hired hands for others, earning hard currency—not rubles—and learning to adjust to a much higher standard of living provided by dollars, deutsche marks, pounds sterling, and francs.

The young Ukrainian navigator, Vladimir Pimenov, and I hit it off right away. While Louie Miller took command, guiding us safely up the pass toward the river, Vladimir offered to show me around the ship. While walking toward the captain's cabin for a peek inside, we passed by the galley. The most distinctive difference between this ship and the one I had come down on just hours before was not of the eye but of the nose! Russian cooking is not Greek cooking! The Greeks have a more elaborate style of eating. It is more varied, with more subtle flavors. The Russians, on the other hand, focus mainly on taking in calories. For them food is nothing fancy, it's just fuel.

We were back on the bridge in time to look out from seven stories high at a beautiful sunrise that looked like the colors of a runny watercolor palette. On the Gulf, the oil platforms glistened, and there were silhouettes of long-legged birds balanced on thin branches. What a spectacular view for those who see it daily and what a price they pay to savor it. The beauty can be overshadowed by long hours, a resentful sea, and separation from family for six months at a time. The good food and high pay is small reward for these relatively young men with old men's responsibilities.

While enjoying the sunrise, a Russian breakfast appeared featuring sausage, sliced tomatoes, cucumber, dark bread, and cheese. No finer restaurant could match the mood or view. As I felt more comfortable, subtle things were more apparent. The ship was strictly utilitarian. Though the paint on the outside was rough and weathered, inside it was clean. Everything was orderly, rooms were well made up, things were put away, not scattered around. But the thing I still ponder was the look in the eyes of most of the crew members. There was an intense, though relaxed, look on their faces. Their movements were deliberate, easy, but precise. Speech was low. But, oh those eyes, those piercing eyes had dreamy, thoughtful looks in them with a longing, yearning quality; lonely yet content, ever searching on the horizon...for what? These men of the sea, do they even know? I think only a man of the sea truly knows. But like the commercial fishermen I met on the river or the towboat captains, they don't know how to explain it so anyone really understands. There must be a Siren of the Sea. There are so many hardships to self and family, and so many sacrifices, yet still they go.

8. Pilottown

A weather front was coming in from the north that was expected to bring heavy rain and gusty winds sometime in the next twenty-four hours and was expected to hang on for a few days. It would have to be my last day in Pilottown. Since arriving the day before (could it have been just the day before?) there had been so much going on that I lost track. After a catnap, Louie Miller and I spent the morning talking. This almost-retirement-age man, who climbed the side of ships as if only in his second decade, filled me in on the business and family life of pilots and the changes in the job over the years. Like a cat circling in on its feeding bowl, he moved closer to me. The ice of the previous evening had melted and transformed into a soothing spring of mateship.

As we spoke, others dropped in. Larry and Dan Myers and then Dave Smith. He suggested I should go down to the post office and talk to his mom, Edna Smith, the postmistress. She was full of history and stories, he said. She had been born there eighty-five years ago and had been at the post office since her husband died in 1960. I walked to the post office down Pilottown's "Main Street," which was actually one of a series of concrete walkways. There were no roads in Pilottown. There were no roads leading to Pilottown, either. The only way in and out was by boat.

Edna Smith was all business as the mail was about to arrive. They got a lot of mail for the ships by general delivery. When the ships finally arrived, they unloaded the mail off the ships at Pilottown where it headed back home to families all over the world.

Edna said the mail got to her a little later as the months had gone by, making her think the mailman must have had a "girlfriend" who delayed him. She was also having to get used to the new boat he had. It didn't sound the same as the old one, and she didn't hear it coming, which was upsetting! As she talked about her life in Pilottown, she canceled letters by hand and bagged the outgoing mail. Her father worked for the bar pilots; he took care of the light across the river and took the weather report on the telephone. The light in those days was a kerosene wick lamp that needed a lot of maintenance, including trimming the wick, cleaning the chimney, and having to row over there every night to light it, sometimes more than once if it blew out.

The houses were all built on pilings four to six feet high to keep them out of the water that sometimes flows under them during storms and high water. The water also flowed under houses in normal conditions when it was forced over the "banks" by a passing ship, if the ship was large enough. Some of the yards were mowed. Others had been let go to be filled with a plant locally called "elephant ears." There must be some risk in doing yard maintenance in Pilottown. I saw a lawn mower beside a house that had a life vest slung over the handle. Until just a short time before my trip, each house had been responsible for its own water, which was gathered from the tin roof and piped into large cisterns built close by. Now there was a central system that gathered water from the roofs of large buildings, treated it, then piped it to the houses in plastic pipe that laid on top of the boardwalk.

Hurricanes Betsy and Camille (1965 and 1969) made some permanent changes here. They blew away twenty-some houses that were never rebuilt, and some people moved away for good. But the hurricanes had also produced some benefits. After the storms Pilottown got a concrete walkway, a central water system, a new power plant, and the pilot headquarter buildings.

"Oh, we have everything now," Edna said. "All the taxes of the big towns but none of the services: no sewer, no garbage pickup, no police. We do it all, but pay their taxes."

In addition to the pilot offices, there was an old school, the post office, some maintenance buildings, and about twenty houses, which were small by our standards. They had just the necessities with a large screened-in porch around three, and sometimes four, sides to offer some protection from the small, but painful, mosquitoes. There were no stores in Pilottown. All supplies came from Venice or New Orleans. There was a diesel generator for electricity and communication—that's done by ship radio or microwave telephone. The mail came daily from Venice, weather permitting, by eleven in the morning to a mobile home that served as their post office. Other deliveries were made by informal means—no brown trucks here! When stuff arrived, it was carried or loaded on old balloon-tire bicycles for the final leg of its journey. I think I saw one of those high-wheeled garden wagons available to deliver heavier items.

Before the hurricane, there was some high farmground where cattle were raised. There was ship loading at the Texaco tanks, some barge loading, and some fishing.

"I guess there were about fifty people and the children at school made about twenty more. Why, one of the teachers here could read stories in the original Greek language, but the school closed when David's kids went up the river to high school. Yeah, they took the boat up to Venice every day for school."

The pages of my notebook were turning as if the wind was blowing them, taking all this down.

"Let's see, today, excluding the pilots, the only ones who still live here are Harvey Cane; David and Marlene and their two kids; Earl and Claude; Russell and his wife, Lorraine; Rodney and his wife and new baby; Gloria and Milton—he cooks for the river pilots and she cooks for the bar pilots...."

I think it was Edna's cousin who had twelve children. Edna's comment about her was troubling to me. She raised these children and the grandchildren, her husband died and now, Edna said, "she can enjoy life." Edna said that before the hurricanes, there were lots of orange trees down there. When they were in bloom, the ship pilots could smell them clear up on the bridge of the ship and did not always know what they were smelling. Today, few of the pilots have permanent homes in Pilottown. Many live in Venice or New Orleans, closer to schools, modern conveniences, and roads.

Dean finally arrived a little late with the mail. "He got a love in his life, that's what," Edna grumbled, as she got to the business of sorting it all out. I left her in her blizzard of white envelopes for a little more time with the pilots.

▼

As evening came, I went down to the river to take in as much as I could. I took a few more rides on the pilotboats as they delivered and retrieved bar and river pilots. Later, I sat on the end of the dock, watching the piers. There were little riffles in the water as it flowed around going down toward the Gulf. But as a big ship came up, these riffles would stop and they would slowly go the other direction as the ship pushed the water upstream. The water level rose as ships passed, sometimes six inches, then returned to its normal level and its standard southerly flow after the ship continued toward New Orleans. It was quite a sight, but nothing more than a practical lesson in physics right at your feet. A seventy-thousand-ton ship displaces seventy thousand tons of water. At around eight pounds per gallon, that's about fifteen million gallons of water that has to go someplace.

Louie came by to suggest that I stay at his house for the night and get a good night's sleep for an early start in the morning. But he wondered whether I should wait longer, until the weather settled.

"Oh, it might be a couple of days," he said. "There's plenty of food and a roof over your head. Better than taking a chance with that little boat. You know discretion is always the better part of valor and you've made it this far. Why push it?"

He was going out to a ship but would be back before I left in the morning. He took me to his little house on pilings where he made sure I had everything and felt at home, then he left to get his ship.

One more time I walked the length of town on its boardwalk, listening to night set in. I passed a bush of Confederate roses, the ones that have pink and white and red blooms on them, and swatted a couple of the tiny mosquitoes that have a stinger that feels like a red-hot needle. Along the way, Captain Svenson and one of the apprentice pilots were out for a walk. I heard a little of their conversation in our few short steps in passing. It seemed the apprentice was having growing pains and second thoughts about his ability to make sound decisions out on those big ships by himself. The captain showed much concern toward this young man, who seemed to be struggling with self esteem more than good judgment.

I had a good dinner, then went to sleep. Tomorrow would be spent backtracking up the Mississippi. Would the current be as bad as those prophets of doom up north had told me? In twelve hours, I would know.

▼

The morning was beautiful with not much wind and a wisp of fog just clearing with a Midwest blue sky overhead. As usual, many told me, "Better have plenty to eat this morning. Take some with you if you like. You sure you want to leave? You could get caught in that storm that's coming. You're more than welcome to stay."

"I'll be all right, it's only forty miles to Empire," I said. As if they didn't know.

And there was Louie, the quiet and reserved captain, the man who shied away when I mentioned I was writing about this trip, the grand old pilot who seemed the least approachable person in Pilottown when I arrived. Now he was telling me all those last-minute things you just don't want to forget. And he had his camera around his neck. He helped put the last few things in the boat and handed the last line over. As I idled away, his camera was clicking and his hand waved a final farewell.

9. A Night in Empire

Coming back up the river I didn't use the charts. These were now familiar waters. There was no sign of bad weather yet, but it was still early in the day, just a little before noon. The doomsayers were wrong this time. It did not take a lot of gas going upriver if you rode the slack water. In the slack water, I hardly noticed the current. With time on my side, I beat the storm to Empire. As I was tying up, Jimmy and Fish, whom I met on my first pass through Empire, came out to greet me. Jimmy warned me about the storm and offered me shelter in his pole shed. I set up my tent, took some food in, put stuff away in the boat, and checked the lines one more time. The sky gave no indication of a storm—still a Midwest blue and just light breezes and a very comfortable seventy degrees.

▼

Empire was more of a trading center and repair station than a typical town. There was a grocery store, a post office, a tavern, and a restaurant, but most of the businesses were related to the fishing industry—processing and wholesaling. Besides the Empire Machine Works, which repaired diesel engines, there was also a hardware and boat supply store just behind the fuel dock at Delta Marina. It reminded me of an old-time store. It was small, filled to the gills, and had aisles so narrow you could hardly get down them and so high you could not see what was on the top. There was little in plastic blister packs; most things were loose in bins or stacked.

As I wandered around, looking here and there, I found it was as well-stocked as any marina. The difference was there was no carpet on the floor and there were no designer items. Chrome was out, and galvanized was in. Gum boots were shrimp white, not yuppie yellow. It was a workingman's boat store. The stuff was used to make a living on the water, not for having a good time. The prices were also more in line with a work store. No one was paying for a name or for status, they were paying for use, plain and simple. Prices for items were about one-third the cost of the same item in a yuppie designer version.

Out in the yard, the skiff *Saint Anthony* was getting its bottom painted by its owner, a tall, proud, light-complicated Yugoslavian named…"Oh, it doesn't matter, you can't pronounce it anyway," he said. "Friendship. That's what counts. Let's just be friends for a while. Stick around, OK?"

Since I never knew his name, we'll just call him "George." He came to the United States some twenty-five years ago—half a lifetime for him. In that time, "George" had not thoroughly learned to read English and his spoken command of it was whimsical and musical. He showed me around his boat. The tapes for his stereo system were Wagner, Strauss, Rachmaninoff, and Beethoven. It was a clean boat; not just orderly, but clean, inside and out. He worked without gloves. He could not get "the feel" with gloves even though his bare hands were wet and cold. You had to have "the feel" to do good work.

His main job that day was painting the bottom of his boat. This is an annual ritual for saltwater boats. To have a fuel-efficient and nimble-handling craft, the bottom must be smooth and clean. This desired state is hindered by various marine growths, both vegetable and animal. The paint not only protects the bottom, but additives in the paint, such as copper, a mild poison, keep it clean of growths. As George opened up, he told me about himself and about the business of oystering around Empire. Though it was not what we in corn country might imagine it to be, there were more similarities than differences between corn farming and oyster farming. One exception, obviously, is that they use boats in place of tractors. Oyster farmers had to have a fishing hole or a dredging bed for a more or less predictable catch. These beds were not just go-fishing places, as you might think. They were just like farmers' fields, staked out and surveyed, and leased from the government for an oysterman's exclusive use, similar to the way grazing rights work out west. These leases had been in the same families for generations and few are on the market for newcomers. In fact, none were. There were waiting lists and outsiders almost never got access—although sometimes big dollars would open a way to a sublease from some old-time holder. Buying a lease was like buying a seat on the New York Stock Exchange. It was way overpriced, but take it or leave it.

It was not really much different in some ways from farming in Iowa. It was comparable to a Midwest farm that's been in a family for years. The younger generation can inherit the land and make some money. But a newcomer buying the same land for fifteen hundred dollars an acre would have a hard time trying to pay for it with corn at two dollars a bushel. As the prices for oysters had gone from twenty-seven dollars per bag the year before to eight dollars, it was getting harder for him to make enough to cover expenses of around $37,000 a year.

An average day for George was nine hours travel and two hours of dredging, then the time it took to sell his oysters, clean up, and prepare for the next day. Most days were overnighters to cut expenses, unless the catch was exceptional.

The dredging beds were only part of the story. During part of the season, fishermen go to the open areas of the Gulf where there are no leases and dredge small oysters to bring to their lease spots. They "bed" these small oysters—or as we would say in the Midwest, "plant" them—to grow to size for a new harvest a few years later. When the oysters were not being harvested, many of these men re-rigged their boats and went out for shrimp. These oystermen were so much like Iowa farmers who have valuable land, expensive machinery and buildings, and who can't always make ends meet but won't quit. Oystering was a way of life for them, and there was much more involved than mere dollars.

It was getting to be late afternoon. The weather was definitely looking stormy and there was a cool, damp feel to the air. George was ready to put the bottom paint on the next day if the weather was OK. For now, he was ready to go home, and I was ready to get something to eat. I walked to the town's only restaurant hoping for a sample of local food, and I was not disappointed. The special was a Cajun version of spaghetti with tomato sauce, shrimp, and Cajun seasoning.

▼

Back at the marina, the approaching storm had encouraged a gathering of some fishermen over foam cups of the local favorite, Richard's Wild Irish Rose Wine with alcohol 18 percent by volume. The volume increased their volume until the place was filled with a mix of English and Cajun French, telling stories of old victories and reluctant defeats, loves that never were and those that could have been, and alas, those that were.

As the scene unfolded, a culture was opened to me in bits and pieces. Here, there was an interesting twist on patriotism. They loved their country, but detested its government. They do all they can to stay away from it and to keep it away from them. One example was the way they did business. In the days of the "cashless society," they dealt mainly in cash that the credit-card culture can't trace; they left no paper trail of their business activities. They told stories of boats worth hundreds of thousands of dollars being paid for out of suitcases of money and tales of the Frigidaire being the most popular maker of strongboxes for home use. On the back bar were two wooden boxes. In them, were receipt books where the few records of business transactions were kept. The bar, in a strange way, was the local financial planner and the barometer of the economic health of the community.

The sun was going down, the bar was closing, the storm was just about here, and it was time for me to go to my home away from home. The wind was coming up from the southwest—not gusty, just a real steady blow. Thunder and lightning filled the sky. Then the rain began, not gradually, but with a vengeance. That tin roof above me was sure welcome. About an hour later, the rain slowed a bit and the wind subsided, switching to a more westerly direction. Seemingly out of nowhere, I got an urge to check my boat.

The water had risen two feet, and I had tied the boat so it wouldn't bang around. In doing so, I didn't leave much slack in the lines in case the water starting rising. When I got there, *Dulcinea* was tipped and swamping. I waded out on the dock that itself was now under about five inches of water. Another couple of inches and I would have had a sunk boat. Thank goodness for my electric pump. Still, the rain was cold and steady and I needed to loosen the lines and retie them with more slack to hopefully avoid tipping for the rest of the night. I tried to work quickly to get out of the biting rain, but it wasn't easy struggling with icy fingers to loosen the wet knots. After letting the bilge pump run for a few minutes, I waded back, soaking wet from head to toe. Back in the tent, I put on some dry clothes and stretched out for the night. Sleep was coming on when headlights shone through the tent and a voice called out.

"Mark…Mark!…Are you there? Are you OK? This is Jimmy. I brought a hamburger and some French fries. Hey, Mark, are you in there?"

Dagwood Bumstead could not have raided the refrigerator in grander style; a hamburger crossed with a submarine sandwich was warm in my stomach, and I was cozy in a sleeping bag out of the storm.

10. Saints and Sole Savers

In the morning, I made a squishy walk to the fuel dock in my shoes, wet from my boat rescue the night before, to check on *Dulcinea* and on the weather forecast. Fish stood at the fuel pump wearing a long, white, flowing robe with a halo over his head. Jimmy, who was launching the Asians' high-powered bateaus, was dressed as a convict. I should not have been surprised. It was Halloween.

The wind had dropped and the water was back to normal. The bay we were on was not very deep—ten feet or so—and it was between five and fifteen miles across, which made it vulnerable to wind. Jimmy told me the water level can vary three feet or more with nobody paying any attention. With a good blow, the water level rises or falls depending on the direction of the wind.

Farther down the dock, I ran into an ol' boy I saw when I arrived the day before. Amid the bustle of boats coming in to avoid the big storm, he calmly watched the skies, nonchalantly sucking oysters. On this day, he was talkative, passing on information and stories. "The fishing industry is highly regulated, you know. Not the freedom to just go fishing out in all that water that sloshes around."

The boats are regulated, the people in them, the equipment they use, and how and when and where it is used. There are pollution regulations and laws to obey. These regulations that are designed to be protective for the insiders are restrictive for the outsiders.

There is a general level of pollution to contend with, which affects the size of the catches and their suitability for sale. Every baby born in Minneapolis contributes to the pollution, as does the new parking lot built in Des Moines, the fertilizer put on a corn field in De Kalb, Illinois, and the lawn in Memphis that just got sprayed with chemicals. It all eventually winds up in the lower Mississippi and the Gulf of Mexico, contributing to the ways of fishing in Empire. Whether we want to recognize it or not, we are all linked together in many ways.

▼

With the exception of slides, tape recordings and notes, I don't collect many souvenirs. One of those exceptions was the result of my wet shoes from the night before. Fish had been watching me and finally interjected that if I didn't want to get sick, I needed to get something dry on my feet.

"You keep your hands and feet dry and warm, that's the best way to stay healthy." (If you do get sick down here, the old standby to get you back and going is the mustard plaster.) Fish pointed to his own feet, down below his angel robes. "You need some of these. They keep your feet dry and you won't get sick. Go over to the store, tell them Fish sent you. They'll take care of you."

And that's how I was introduced to the fourteen-inch high, shrimp-white, non-slip, gum-soled boots that every waterman down here wears. The ones I got were not the favorite—the ones made in Colombia with the tan sole. I got the Red Balls with a wider toe. In them, you wear a heavy wool sock and fit the boots so that they are easy to kick off quickly. This gives them the characteristic "waterman's scuffing" sound when walking. They called them "Cajun Reeboks." But in street language, they were known as "coon-ass sneakers."

The term "coon ass" caught me off guard when I first heard it. I thought it was a bigoted, redneck retaliation against another subculture. However, I learned that the Cajuns refer to themselves and things of their culture, at times, as "coon ass." It was something like the experience I had in Australia, where the word "bastard," or as they pronounce it, "baah-sturd," is a common adjective.

Depending on how you say it, it could land you on your back with a fist stuffed up your nostrils or a laugh and the hug of an ol' mate. These endearments can be misunderstood from the outsider's perspective, in that they have the common thread of both degradation or adulation, depending on their context.

I walked back to the docks and showed Fish my new "coon-ass" sneakers. He smiled with approval. "Now you'll stay healthy—won't get a cold from wet feet." Fish earned the halo he wore that day.

▼

I wanted to try to find someone to ask about a better place to stay when I got back to New Orleans. I didn't want to stay on Lake Pontchartrain as I did before because high winds could trap me in the city again. At the same time, I wanted to stay somewhere safe. New Orleans did not strike me as the safest city in the world. While walking through the boats, I ran into a Coast Guard officer and his men, who were on patrol. This group was not like the ones in New Orleans. They were more temperate, even friendly. The officer was understanding when I asked him about a place to stay in New Orleans. He agreed that bad weather could trap me at Lake Pontchartrain and that, yes, my feelings were correct that New Orleans was not that safe, especially for someone in a small boat at night.

"The city's industrial area should be treated with caution," he added, "and it should not even be considered for an overnight spot, unless someone stood watch—there is too much that could (and does) go on there."

He recommended a marina on the Intracoastal Waterway at Chalmette, not far from the city. There, I could tie up next to a motel with several big marinas right on the highway only five miles from New Orleans. The Coast Guard bunch was interested in seeing this boat that brought me all the way here from up north. As they gave it the once-over, their comments were positive. They pointed out things they liked about the boat and said things such as, "You sure are well-equipped." As we looked, the officer in his late twenties, walked to the back of the boat and read the name, "*Dulcinea,*" he paused. "Is that Don Quixote's—"

"Yes it is!"

"His lady in waiting?"

"Yup."

He paused and began to laugh, a real belly laugh. He looked at me. "No offense, but —"

"Don't worry," I replied.

He pointed at the name and said, "You got that right!"

It was the first time I didn't have to explain it all. We explained it to the others, then all had a good laugh. Others out of earshot hadn't a clue. What fun!

▼

Sometime during the night, a sailboat had been towed in from seventy miles out in the Gulf. They had lost a shaft and had been in some serious trouble. The crew found a place to stay and were waiting for repairs the next day so they could get back on their way as soon as possible. In the meantime, they were at the bar with the locals sharing their misfortune and a brew all around.

On the bar's television, the important focal point was a football game between the New Orleans Saints and some other insignificant team that was just going to get beat, or so the talk went. That sentiment was not unanimous, though, as there was some betting going on. As they watched the tube and drank, they nibbled on hard-boiled and pickled eggs.

Just then a voice boomed, "Hey, where's the shrimp Jimmy? Hey, this'll never do! Somebody got some shrimp?"

A voice answered from the bar, "I'll get some." He left and returned in a few minutes with a white plastic five-gallon bucket more than half full, fresh off his boat. From behind the bar, Jimmy emerged with a shrimp boiler and a large aluminum pot that he set out on the concrete slab by the front door. One man had a hose to fill the pot, while another added a potato, a piece of sausage, an ear of corn, and salt. In little more time than it would take to pop a batch of popcorn, the pot was full of boiling water with the spices added, and the shrimp quickly followed. It was watched with careful eyes that were washed for clear vision with Richard's Red-Eye Wash.

Inside, the bar was carefully prepared for the delicacy. Old newspaper was spread out in several layers the length of the bar, topped with several more layers of the "quicker-picker-upper," where the boiled-to-perfection shrimp were unceremoniously spread on top in a long windrow. The prescribed Cajun etiquette is, "Dig in!" You peel the skin off with your fingernails, throw the skins on the floor, where they will be swept up later, relax, and enjoy the game on TV. Just the simple life.

11. Translations

The next morning, I headed back up to New Orleans, passing through the old locks at Empire at about seven in the mornings. Today, the lockmaster was the old lockmaster's son, who was studying to be a Baptist preacher. His work days were used as his study hall for homework from the seminary. We waved a good-bye for my short trip up the river. I arrived at the industrial lock about eleven in the morning. By one o'clock the boat was tied up and Tom was on his way to get me. The slip I tied up to at Chalmette was not more than one hundred feet from the road and ten feet from the drive into the motel office.

I planned to stay with Tom and Judy for a couple of days to finish up the projects we had started, do a little last-minute shopping, and take in some sightseeing. But more important, I made arrangements for venturing up the bayous.

The return route was to be the one I was encouraged to use coming down, only in reverse—a 150-mile trip, twisting and turning through Cajun Country on the Intracoastal Waterway. From New Orleans, I would head south and west to Houma, then west toward Morgan City, north paralleling the Mississippi past Plaquemine, then east again to Port Allen, which is just across the river on the west bank from Baton Rouge. Finally, I would wind up at Cargo Carriers in Port Allen, where I would leave the boat while going north to get the truck and trailer to bring it back to Des Moines (which was some nine hundred highway miles away).

It was hard to believe the trip was coming to a close. It was even harder to think about having to slip back into "everyday living" again. It does get tiring on the go, but you get used to that ever-changing view at your window.

▼

My last night in New Orleans was spent at a patio dinner with Diane, Phil, and Lars. Diane is Tom's business partner, Phil is her husband and Lars is her first cousin once removed—Lars' father and Diane's grandfather were brothers in their native Norway. As the evening progressed, Diane mentioned that she had some old letters upstairs that her father had written to her mother when they were courting at home in the old country. Of course, they were written in the old way and in Norwegian. She always wished she knew what they said to each other, to sort of eavesdrop on a romance in the making.

"Get 'em," Lars said. "I think we can figure them out." He was in his late sixties or early seventies, so he could translate not only the foreign language, but also the old-fashioned nuances that revealed the emotions of the letters for his modern audience. Diane flew to get the letters. Lars put on his half-frame cheaters and pondered the old, faded pages. They were written with a dip pen, and the shadings of the writer's hand were evident. A romance of long ago was brought to life again at that table. By our standards, it was stiff. But by the standards of the day and what you dared to put in writing, they were full of pure young love from a Norwegian man to his sweetheart.

Diane had tears in her eyes. She never knew her father could have expressed such feelings. There was the custom of much public restraint in their culture. Even Lars was struck. This was not removed from his past but a few years and I think there were memories of his own feelings with his own sweetheart just a few years departed. The wine we drank that night was a good buffer for those flowing emotions.

▼

On November 3, after all the odds and ends were finished up in New Orleans, I left for Cajun country. You never go through New Orleans in a hurry. They don't do things that way. It's not a Southern laid-back attitude, but an attitude common to seaport societies with indifference and contrived attention to detail, a lot of cynicism, and few loyalties except to thyself. It took three hours to go through two locks and travel five miles of river to get to the Harvey Ship Canal, across from New Orleans proper. It seemed that they made me wait sometimes for no reason—just a chance to wield their absolute power as ruthlessly as possible.

At the Harvey Locks I was told that I would have to wait a few minutes since the lockmaster was "indisposed." Translation: He had to go to the bathroom. At least this was a reason I could understand, so I didn't mind waiting for the lockmaster to return and open the gates to the waterway that would lead to Cajun land.

PART V
CAJUN LAND

1. Adapt and Survive

There was no sudden change on the other side of the lock in the Harvey Canal. There was plenty of ship building, oil field equipment, exploration equipment, and even a small submarine hanging on a crane to be loaded. But there was a dramatic change about five miles down the canal and it came like crossing the border into Mexico. It happened when I left the Harvey Canal and joined the Intracoastal Waterway.

The water abruptly changed from a clear waterway to one speckled with water lilies. There were enough to cause a stop every so often to tip the engine up and pull wound-up stems from the prop. The water was clear and smelled good. There were sounds of the bush, not of man. There was no apparent current, just a gentle, straight channel about two hundred feet wide and lined with trees on both sides. Every so often, there were signs of houses set back in the swamp; little settlements of a dozen dwellings with roosters crowing; out buildings and boats tied along the banks.

A few miles out was a settlement of weekend homes, for the people from the big city. For a twist, there were some very luxurious homes mixed right in there with the weekend camp retreats with bateaus tied beside the big skiffs.

The destination for the day was Lafitte, or Jean Lafitte, depending on who you asked or what map you looked at. It is a bayou town twenty-five or thirty miles by road from New Orleans.

The town is laid out along the bayou. The road came later, much later. It is believed the pirate Lafitte was active in the area and is possibly buried in the cemetery there by the junction of the bayous just north of town.

I tied up at the town's northern outpost, a general store, hardware store, and fuel dock for passersby. This was one of those places that had the feel of an old-time feed store where there was more than just business carried on. It was a clearinghouse for local gossip and a game of cards. I gathered information there on things to look at and a good place to sample Cajun's Cajun food. They told me about a place called Boutte's, which had a parking lot for those who drove there and a dock for those who floated by on the bayou.

"You can't miss it. Just pass the bridge on the left bank about five miles down," I was told.

Inside Boutte's was a mix of locals and people who had driven from New Orleans for a more relaxed atmosphere. The special for the day was crawfish étouffée, a thick rice-based soup with crawfish and spices. It wasn't fire hot, but it was definitely spicy! The only English I heard was from the outsiders; all the locals spoke Cajun. Even on the radio the DJ, the music, and the commercials were all in Cajun. Maybe I did cross a border.

I tried to read the menu as I waited, but the only items that were recognizable were Coke, Sprite and milk. The rest was in French. Looking out the window, the boats were all of a different flavor, good looking with beautiful lines. Even the small bateaus were different. The ones that stood out were the "gringo" boats; the others were Cajun. This was the land of the famous Lafitte skiff, an all-purpose boat that has evolved over the years to its present form. Over the years it might evolve into something else for that is the Cajun way, adapt and survive.

It's amazing Cajun culture and tradition has survived. Beginning back in 1755, they came to Louisiana as refugees of British atrocities, at least that's the way the media would categorize them if it happened today. The Acadians were French-descended settlers in British territory in what is now Eastern Canada. When they refused to vow allegiance to England, British soldiers expelled them; many came to the bayous. Over the years, their people's name was adapted from Acadian to Cajun. Since settling in Louisiana, Cajuns have become an ethnically mixed and very self-sufficient stock. They shun outside help beyond immediate family or the extended family at the most. The community parish church is the absolute furthest that the older Cajuns go for help.

Cajuns have been adaptable to whatever has come their way over many years. Sometimes these changes result in compromises that contradict their beliefs. The church in the lower parishes, as with the Mayans in Mexico, seems to survive only with the blessing of the Voodoo Queen.

▼

That night I learned of a local named Bobby Boudreaux. To some, he was a legend in his own time when it came to building a skiff; I was definitely going to look for him the next day. Meanwhile, I had a lot to prepare for the trip ahead. I had to get fuel, clean up, and then go to the grocery store.

Another boat was tied up beside me now, a fifty-footer on the way back to Houston. The couple who owned it were in a hurry to get back from their summer home in Florida to check on their business. They were concerned the present administration in Washington was out to take all their money away from them. We walked together to the store about six blocks, where the conversation followed the same theme.

"The produce is not of the same quality and the prices are now outrageous, we have stopped here on the way for the last nine years and every year it gets worse," they said.

That night as I ate my gourmet can of Dinty Moore stew, my smeller was distracted by the aroma from the rack of barbecued ribs in the smoker on the fantail of their fifty-footer next to me. The next morning was the same. I couldn't smell my oatmeal simmer. Their fried potatoes, sausage and eggs overpowered it, as they motored away with those new twin 250-horsepower Perkins diesels silently propelling them home.

2. Craftsmanship

First thing in the morning, I checked out Bob's Net Shop, which was just a short walk around the corner. The building was off the main road on the banks of the bayou with its own dock. The building was a cedar no-painter with residents living upstairs and the shop below. There was lots of open floor space and high ceilings. Around the edge were bins of parts including hooks, line cleats, eye bolts, gimbals, and things I couldn't identify. Overhead were sheaves and blocks of all sizes, from little ones you could put in your shirt pocket to those you could not wrap with your shirt. Somewhere overhead were spools of rope in storage, but all you could see was the ends of rope hanging through holes, handy to pull off what was needed. At one end of the room were big spools of light cordage—or maybe super-heavy kite string—the raw material for fishnets or trawls.

Bob was a young man, with dark hair and eyes, that had a certain spark to them. Bob and his father worked together in a way. Bob sold the rigging to furnish the boats to pull the fish in and his father sold the boats. His father was Bobby Boudreaux.

"He is just this side of the bridge," Bob said. "You can't miss it!"

Bobby's boatyard was a collection of wrinkled, rusted, metal buildings from the edge of the water to a couple hundred feet back. There was a small dock that no respectable sailor would ever willingly tie to for an extended stay. The man was an eccentric or an artist and likely both. He was my kind of man. There was nothing superfluous there. There was a roof to keep the sun and rain off and the remnants of walls to keep most of it from blowing in. There were no signs. Everyone who needed him knew where he was. There was no carpet on the floor in his office; it was easier not having to wipe your boots off. The phone hung high on the wall out of the way alongside a kitchen clock, which no one seemed to pay much attention to and whose hands pointed in directions that had no relation to the "real" time. Work orders were scratched in Cajun shorthand on salesmen's promotional scratch pads and filed away under nuts and washers on the table or hung on eightpenny nails driven in the wall. Rooms that once held stacks of selected boat wood, now contained barrels of polyester resin, rolls of matting, cans of solvent, and vials of catalyst, the raw materials for newer fiberglass boats. On the floor lay tools, vapor masks, and rags in the corner. If someone walked in with a lighted smoke in their teeth, it would be Hiroshima all over again. Gosh, I felt at home!

When I got there, the master was away. The two apprentices were busy at work on a custom boat out in one of the sheds. Their appearance was a poor reflection of their skills. They wore coveralls so stiff they reminded me of the Tin Man, and they had a laid-back attitude that could put some to sleep. But never mind any of that, they were creating works of art. High on blocks was one of the most graceful hulls I had seen. It looked like it was more a part of the water than something that was to be put in it. The lines were smooth; the workmanship was masterful, akin to fine cabinet work.

Bobby did not show up for a little while. In the meantime, those guys went out of their way to explain what was going on and to tell a little history. Bobby was a fisherman, like the rest, who became dissatisfied and started fiddling with his own ideas. Before long, his fishing days were limited and he found himself too busy building boats for others. In those days, he used wood. He didn't have a formal education or schooling in naval architecture or any idea how to draw and loft a design; he just laid out the keel the length you wanted and filled in the details.

His boats were not only nice to look at, they were seaworthy, and with the proper power in them, they were fast. Five hundred horsepower Cat engines were the favorite there, and some boats had a pair of engines to push them along even faster. There were a few around that when fully rigged could easily plane at thirty knots! Bobby no longer took the risk of going to sea every day. He stayed at home on land building boats for those who went to sea and put some jingle in his pocket for his effort. The big boat under the shed was an example of what those who have the bucks buy. The boat was a "yacht" version of a workboat—$100,000 bare, plus $40,000 for a pair of 435-horsepower Cat engines to push it.

Years ago, when he was still a starving craftsman, some guys came down from the "big city," representing one of the big boatyards and showed interest in his work. They "generously" offered to help him make the transition from wood to fiberglass construction. If he let them use one of his hulls as a plug for them to make a mold, they would train him in fiberglass construction and give him a hull for a starter. What they did, in effect, was give him three dollars for a hit song. He made the transition and recovered nicely. In fact, his boats were in such demand that he lived in the largest, grandest house on the bayou. Yet, success never changed him and his focus never wavered. He was still a feeling artisan. What counted most was not the appearance of the boatyard but the product. It was the boat, always the boat! He had the master's touch. His shop showed it. Just a place to create—he needed nothing more.

As the apprentices finished telling me Bobby's story, a burgundy Cadillac (with ashtray still empty) drove up and disgorged a tall, fiftyish, bearded, old kid wearing high-top sneakers, jeans and three shirts in layers topped by a plaid flannel with the shirttail flapping. He pushed his fists in his pockets and this old James Dean spring-heeled across the yard to the boat where we stood, cocked his head, and glanced an approving eye around.

3. Spirits and Wakes

Most boats of significance have some sort of ensign on their mast. Until then, I had none, but that morning, I had one of the finest of them all. From the antenna on the bow the glorious gossamer work of a spider was flowing in the breeze, covered with little micro-spheres of dew, glistening like silver and crystal, trailing fifteen feet in the air currents almost the length of the boat. What a way to be led through the morning!

As I left for Houma, the tide was coming in and the flow of the waterway had changed. The water lilies were going upstream. It is a characteristic of a bayou—it flows in both directions. Around the bend, I passed the cemetery with its leaning elaborate tombstones topped with Catholic crosses and deep-relief carvings that cast shadows. I thought, "Whose spirit would be with me this day?"

There was a stretch of the bayou just around the bend from the cemetery that had been laid out by surveyor's instruments, not by the whims of nature. It was straight for miles. These straight stretches gave me time for meditations. I wondered what had happened to Merle, the man in the kayak back on the Mississippi. He was going my way, and I had backtracked to New Orleans and had lost track of him. No one else had seen him after Burnside, just up the river from New Orleans. There had always been comments that people disappear out there on the river. Had he disappeared on the river, gotten off the river, or did he disappear in the river. All along the way he had been noticed, yet now no one had seen him. Merle, where are you?

▼

The charts I used to find my way through the Intracoastal Waterway were seventeen years old. The world Bob Jorgenson saw here when he first used the charts had changed. It was not what he saw. There weren't islands where his charts showed them. Some of the bridges were gone, others had taken their place, and new ones had been built where none existed before. Just outside Houma, I was confused. Where there was supposed to be a crossing of channels was a large shallow lake that in places was strewn with stumps. I was to learn that this was the result of a fire a few years back. As I understood it, the vegetation never grew back, and then erosion started to wash away the soil. There were many more little settlements along the way than the seventeen-year-old map showed—changes even here in the backwaters on the same scale as the suburbs of mid-America.

▼

In 1989, I went through Houma on my motorcycle when I was going from Key West to the Arctic. This time, I was not seeing it by road but by water, and it did not look the same. The city was locally known as the Venice of Louisiana. It was crisscrossed with canals and waterways. I had to go under five bridges to get to my destination. The bridges on the Intracoastal Waterway were all high enough for normal traffic to go under, although some were draw-bridges that could be raised and lowered for taller boats. But some side canals, including Bayou Terrebonne which I was taking, had low-lift bridges, not more than a few feet above the water. As I slipped under them, there was only about three inches of clearance. I ducked below the top of the little helm that held the charts. If I needed the bridge to be lifted, I'd have to make a phone call and wait half an hour for the bridgekeeper to arrive. With budget restraints, bridgekeepers were cut down to a roving band who traveled as needed rather than a bridgekeeper for each bridge sitting in one place all day.

After leaving the main canal, the Terrebonne runs through an industrial and business area. Then in transition, it finds its way to the residential neighborhoods, where I was headed. I was looking for the Whitneys' house where I had stayed back in 1989. I wondered if I would recognize their house after all this time. I never anticipated I would have to remember it, even though they had invited me back. Again, so much for never saying never. And never did I ever think I would return by water! But sure enough, there it was.

There were plenty of places to tie to the bank. Now things looked familiar as I came over the bank, and looked across the road. They were out picking fall flowers and pecans. Under the trees was the spot I had set up camp the first time. Elmay spotted me.

"Haw! We been waitin' fur ya! Haw ya beeen? Where ya got ya boat? Oh, dat's not da beeest place to leave it, the area deeeteriorated since ya beeen here. We gon' have to find 'nother place fur ya. Bernard, ya call down there to them to see if he can leave it with them fur a couple days, OK? Get ya stuff and make ya self at home. Ya know the way!"

Elmay was the missus and Bernard was the mister. They were old-time Cajuns in the area. Her grandfather was a plantation owner in the lower parishes with three hundred slaves at one time. Bernard helped me carry stuff over and directed me to where I could tie up. With the boat taken care of, we went back to where I set my tent up not more than a few feet from where it was four years previously.

▼

The next morning looked good with thin clouds and warm temperatures as I headed out. The day's goal was to reach Jack Miller's Store, a trading post on the outskirts of Plaquemine, eighty miles from Houma. Bernard said that at one time Houma was the busiest seaplane center in Louisiana, serving the oil industry. Along the sides of the canal, there were still quite a number of them pulled up on the banks. Farther from the heart of town, there were planes in backyards, where they were launched to the bayou from ramps that looked just like overgrown boat ramps.

I wondered how much they were still used since helicopters seemed to offer much more versatility. Before I could think too much about that, ahead of me in the canal, a plane pulled out, turned out in the center, and then came straight towards me. It went by, close enough for me to see the pencils in the pilot's pockets. It rose out of the water, slowly gained altitude as it flew under the bridge, and made a slow turn to the right. That answered my question; planes were still used out there. Before long, another plane and I shared the water as it landed. You needed to look for more than fellow boatmen in this town's waterway.

▼

Every so often, everyone needs a wake-up call, just to keep them alert. I got one when I crossed a wide part of the bayou—more of a lake, really. It was wide and shallow and several miles long with no wind protection. There were waves building up to the two-foot level or higher, and I was only about one-fourth of the way across. What looked like the ideal solution was right ahead of me; an ocean tug. Like the Norwegian freighter back on the Mississippi, it was large enough to block the wind and settle the waves a few hundred feet behind it, so I got up behind it for refuge.

We thumbed along at about 6 to 8 mph most of the way across until the wind had gone down and the lake was smooth enough for me to make it on my own and pick up the pace a little. So I dropped back and swung wide to go around, giving myself what I thought was plenty of room to cross his wake in safety, but these ocean tugs are deep-hulled, displace a lot of water, and have tremendous power tucked away. I crossed his wake and looked down from the peak of the wave into what seemed to be a bottomless pit. The boat went down and just at the bottom, another wall of water just a little more than a boat length away went up just as steeply. The bow started to rise, but not fast enough. This was stupid; not a way to end it all in the middle of a bright, sunny day in water not twenty feet deep!

The bow kept rising, but not fast enough. Part of the wave broke over the bow. In less than a second, this wall of water would inundate my boat and sink me. But miraculously, the bow kept rising and *Dulcinea* lifted out and over the top of the wave. On the other side, there weren't any more waves, but I had ankle-deep water sloshing around me making the boat unstable. I have no idea whether I did the right thing, but I gave it full throttle to get the bow up and turned the bilge pump on. The water came to the back of the boat and stayed in one place. The bow was high in case I hit more water. In twenty minutes, the water was gone and I was much wiser!

▼

The next city was Morgan City, another shipbuilding center. I bypassed Morgan City using the inside route going around Lake Palourde on the east side. It was a very picturesque route. The bayou narrowed and there were stretches where the trees tightly lined the bank only a hundred feet across. In other places, a so-called conventional swamp surrounded me. In places, the banks were lined with little settlements, some permanent, others for weekenders. Most were modest. Even this far south, the nature of the trees and other vegetation was changing from the tropical mix of cypress and palmettos to large patches of Southern live oaks and pines.

4. Jay J

At two-thirty in the afternoon I arrived at Jack Miller's Store, a real institution, founded in 1911. Until a few years ago, the place was known as Jack Miller's Landing, and was accessible only by boat with questionable roads not always going anywhere. The store had hunting and fishing supplies along with groceries and health care items.

I found a place to stay at Verret's boatyard, another gathering of nondescript buildings along the banks. I tied up around the end of the barges that served as work docks where two medium-sized pushboats were tied. Murray, as he introduced himself, was the owner of the boatyard. He told me it was going to freeze that night.

"It might be better to stay on the *Jay J* over there—just tell them Murray said it was all right."

Well, it wasn't all right. The occupants of the pushboat said I would have to check with their boss in Baton Rouge. So much for that.

I set up my camp for the night, then went for a walk around town, to the store, and over to the shipyard where there was still activity late this Saturday afternoon. I found out that a boat had lost its rudder and a new one was being made so it could be installed later that day or early the next morning, meaning sometime after midnight and before sunrise. I watched with great respect as these men cut steel and welded wire the size of old coat hangers. When they welded at twenty-nine volts and 300 amps, wire came off the reel like kite string on a March afternoon in the schoolyard.

The workers were Ted Verret (Murray's son) and Dale Lively (Murray's foreman). While I watched, Murray came by.

"I saw your tent," he said. "You must be a glutton for punishment to camp out tonight!" After I told him about the conversation with the boat crew, he just looked at me. "Oh," he said. "Don't worry about that." And with that, he was off.

Even though the rudder they were working on was roughly four by five feet with a five-inch diameter shaft on it, the precision these guys used was unexpected. Though they used a cutting torch to cut it out, they used the tool with the precision of a seamstress' scissors. It didn't have the rough, bubbly, slaggy stuff you see so often on big machinery. It looked like it had been cut with a laser. The welds were the size of the caulking around a loose-fitting window in a tenement house, though they looked more like finely tooled mortar joints.

"It's all settled," Murray said, returning only a few minutes after he had left. "You'll stay on the *Jay J*. Come on over for a hot meal before you go to warm up. We are having duck gumbo and peach cobbler tonight."

▼

Back on the *Jay J* after supper, crew member Phillip Edwards showed me my room for the night. It was one of the crew bedrooms with walls of half-inch steel plate, bunk beds, a heavy wood door, an air conditioner, one smallish light bulb, and no windows.

Sleep was similar to the night I spent in a cave at Coober Pedy, Australia, an old opal-mining town where most people live in dugouts for protection from extreme temperatures. My cave was a motel built by an old miner. In the cave, there was no light or sound and on the *Jay J*, with the exception of the lulling, throbbing generator below, it was the same. It was a secure feeling with a warm stomach full of Cajun gumbo. Heaven!

▼

When I finally found my way out of bed, Phillip, one of the *Jay J's* two crew members, was in the kitchen intently working over a large frying pan. He was making a roux, the base of many of the traditional recipes. There is a saying that reflects the importance and critical timing in making a roux. When you make a roux, you take the phone off the hook, throw the cat out, and send the kids to the neighbors, lest you burn it; so close is a good roux to disaster if done right.

I asked Phillip how to make a good roux. He told me to start out with a seasoned cast iron pan, grease, and flour. When I asked him how much, he said, "You learn by feel. Start out with a little grease and a small fist of flour. Then, heat the pan just enough to melt the grease, then stir the flour in, increasing the heat to brown the flour. Brown the flour to just before it burns for the proper flavor. It's just that simple."

The roux he was making was for the stew for lunch and dinner that day. Phillip looked in the icebox and was a little short on stuff for the stew. He was going to have to make do.

"Hey, do they have that stuff at Jack's store?" I asked. He thought they might, but had no money. "Forget it," I said. "What do you need? I'll see about it."

Three dollars did it—a pepper, some garlic, an onion, and spuds. He cut up a good steak for the beef, peeled some carrots, a bay leaf, red pepper, and black pepper, and Cajun magic. By half past one, he thought we could sample a little, but it would be better by night. The lid went back on that big iron kettle just a little off center to let steam escape so it could simmer down and tempt the nose.

Phillip's mother was Cajun and the best of cooks. When he was young, she told him, "You better learn to cook and take of yourself. These young womens, 'dey no good—too lazy to learn to cook and take care of mens properly." That's how he came to learn to cook—and might I add, quite well for a twenty-three-year-old feller.

He told me how to fix crawdads for gumbos or "any other ways you want them." One popular way is "just shuck 'em and eat 'em 'dat way. The best is if you cook a lot of 'em, they have a better flavor than just a few."

"How many are you talking about, Phillip?"

"Oh, a bag."

"How many is that?"

"Forty pounds. They don't go far with a group of friends around. They just disappear. They only cost about thirty to forty dollars a bag, depending on the market."

Anyway, this is how to do it:

Get a big pot—those aluminum ones that hold about ten gallons are fine—and fill it with water. Put a box of salt in and then the live crawdads. Let them soak a half hour and rinse in cold water. The saltwater causes them to spit up, purging the mud from their insides, for a sweeter taste when cooked. Rinse them a couple of times, then fill the pot again and bring it to a boil. Throw in, some potato chunks, cayenne pepper, salt, garlic, crab boil (a mixture of spices in a package), half an onion, and some halved sweet corn. That will cool the water down, so bring it to a boil again and put the crawdads in—don't wash the fat off the tails, that's where the flavor is. Bring the water to a boil for about ten minutes. Kill the fire and let it set for a half hour with the lid on. They are now ready to eat or to put in something else.

Another favorite that is an adaptation is Cajun turkey or ham. First you make a real thin soup of the following ingredients by running them through a blender by themselves, then all together: garlic, parsley, green onions, celery, and bell pepper. Then, after it is really thin, add salt, black pepper, and red pepper. This soup is not cooked, but injected with a large syringe through the meat very liberally, then it is deep fat fried whole in a big pot of oil, but not just any oil. This is the adaptation to the modern world. The oil must be old, dark oil, from a place like McDonald's. This gives it the distinctive Cajun character.

▼

When the boat was tied at Verret's, Phillip went home at night. The other crew member stayed on the boat. I met him the day before when he came on board. It came out that he was just back on the job. He had some time off in prison. It was never mentioned why, but it was serious. He was now on parole under strict supervision. He was complaining about losing fifty dollars at a card game the night before. This dude was in his late twenties, about six feet tall and well built, with a distant look in his eyes. His voice was gentle in tone and augmented by kindly body language, but his eyes sent a different message.

He stayed on the ship that night and was up when I went to bed. Sometime during the night, he must have gone out because when he woke me up about two in the morning, he was dressed and smelled of cologne. His knock on the door was followed by comments that he was "just out of prison and was lonely." He knew he shouldn't ask me, he said, and that my funds might be limited, but could I help him with twenty or thirty dollars for some companionship? He was young and full of vinegar.

There was a sharp edge on his voice that his eyes usually held. It could have sounded like a request, but to me, at two in the morning, that was not how it sounded, and I wasn't that comfortable with it at all. I used the old man's excuse for time.

"Go on down to the galley. Give me some time to go to the bathroom and I'll see what I can do for you." With some time to think, I made sure the only thing I had was ten dollars in cash. He looked dejected and more than a little disappointed. Thinking a bit, he said, "OK," took it and left.

Since going back to bed would be hard after that, I found my way up to the pilothouse; it was beautiful! It was half past two, and the fog on the bayou was just a wisp, caressing the water's surface like cobwebs floating in the morning air. The sounds coming in the windows were of the swamps, hushed and muffled, although an occasional splash punctuated the otherwise still surroundings. When I first was on the river, way back on the first night out, I had a fear about being on the river at night. Now there was this yearning to be on the river at night to experience those sounds and sights.

The fog was thickening, but I could see over the top of it to the banks. The water, however, was obscured most of the time as the fog drifted by. A two-barge tow slipped by in the fog; the engines hummed quietly. The footsteps of the crew sounded prominently on the steel decks. There was a ring around the moon. Soon the sun began to come up. It was my last day out there. By the end of the day, I would be back at Cargo Carriers in Port Allen getting ready to go north. The sun was putting color in the sky. The slate gray gave way to magenta and gold. Someplace a rooster was crowing. From up in the pilothouse, I saw the fog on the bayou rolling across the top like smoke from an old-time leaf burning in the backyard on a Saturday afternoon as it drifted across the neighbor's yard. The sun was lighting the top of the trees and reflecting on the top of the fog. So much for getting some sleep before I left.

Stuff was packed and I was untying the lines when a work boat pulled in behind me. The men on deck were talking while busy with their docking chores. Their attitude was: "America: Love it or leave it." They complained about immigrants stealing jobs from "real" Americans and about how the glut of inferior imported products destroyed "our way of life," yet they wore made-in-Korea Nikes, made-in-Japan Casio watches, and made-in-Malaysia T-shirts. These men were the kind who would stand and put their hand to their heart as the flag passed. They would object if someone dared to burn the American flag. Yet the flag on their boat was so desecrated with diesel smoke and so worn by the weather that you could not tell the stars from the blue. The red stripes were just a little darker than the white ones. It was so frayed around the edges, with a lacy look, that it would have been more at home as fuel for a fire to signal troops on the bayou.

The boat, by contrast, was sparkling clean. It wasn't dirty or in disarray. So why was the flag so filthy? There were many possibilities. Was it because the crew was distracted and didn't notice the flag, or were they aware of it but couldn't do anything because it was the boatowner's responsibility? Whatever the reason, it looked bad.

The sun was now sparkling though the radio was predicting unsettling weather. It was a good idea for me to take advantage of the weather and leave early.

5. Skippin' Rocks

This part of the bayou seemed to be more primitive as I got closer to Baton Rouge than it had been farther from the big city. The water was settled, the trees were closer and denser; a mystery right at the water's edge. With only about ten miles to go, my mind wandered into reflection. I was glad I went down the Mississippi. I would not have wanted to miss it and never would have wanted to miss the bayous I had been on the past few days. Suddenly, the trees took on a Northern look with fall colors, dropping leaves. The radio must have been right. The sky was starting to cloud up and the air had that tempered feel you get before a storm, though the sun still shone bright through thin horsetails.

The lock was just ahead. Over the radio, the lockmaster advised that it would be forty-five minutes before I could enter, so I pushed up on a bank to wait. The smell and sounds of civilization were in the air. Just three miles back, you would have never known a city was out here. There must be quite a water level change at this lock. As they empty the lock, the water in the bayou rises about six to eight inches and there is a definite current going back the other way. When the gates opened, it was easy to see why the bayou level changed. This is a huge lock, about twelve hundred feet long and maybe a hundred feet wide. I was nothing but a speck in there—just a little foam on the water.

Soon the far gates opened. There was the Mississippi again. Motoring out and around the corner was Cargo Carriers or CCI as they were referred to out there. I pulled around the end of the

Warren Elsey, their floating office, which is the remains of a once-proud steel-hulled, coal-fired, paddle wheel line of boat from the early 1900s. It was still serving a useful life in retirement.

Mel had been expecting me and invited me to his office, then suggested I get the boat taken care of since a storm was coming. It seemed there had been some mix-up—a coal-loading barge and its support boats were taking up the space that I was to use while there. But no matter, that's what friends are for. Mel made a few phone calls, and all was well. Glen McKinney, at McKinney Towing across the river, would take care of the boat, and I would come back and stay on the *Warren Elsey*.

A mile across the river, Glen met me at his dock and surveyed the situation. As the swell from a passing tow bounced me around, he decided I needed a place off the river to put the boat. He called his son on the radio with instructions to get the trailer and meet me at the ramp just up the river. At a quarter past three the boat was out of the water. It was November 8. The first time it was in the water was September 17. The water part of the trip was over! Terry, the captain of the Cargo Carriers crewboat, was on his way over to get me. In his thirty-five-foot aluminum crewboat with twin 400-horsepower engines, he cut through the wake of a passing tow at 25 mph. So my last ride on the river was with Terry on the white CCI crewboat, pounding through waters I had cautiously picked my way through just minutes before.

Back on the *Warren Elsey*, Mel wanted to catch up on what had happened since we last saw each other weeks before. As we talked, John Wilder, his boss, came by.

"Say, it's going to be stormy tonight, why don't you plan to stay in my office up in the old wheelhouse tonight. Better than out on the deck."

I found myself among so many spirits of the past that last night. The wheelhouse was now a carpeted office with all the modern appointments of a desk, couch, telephone, and fax. It was once a bare room with a great wooden wheel, engine room telegraph, bell and whistle ropes; it had no radar or depth sounder—just keen vision and a rope with a weight on it.

There was history all around me that night on the *Warren Elsey*. I walked the center hall and wondered, "Oh, if these walls could talk." This was my last night on the river. What a way to end it. I sat in the darkened room in the wheelhouse, looking out the window at the lightning, watching powerful searchlights probe here and there. The thunder rolled and I felt the water buffet the boat as the storm raged on. Looking out the window during one of the powerful flashes of lightning, I saw across the river. Up on the bank, out of it all at McKinney's, was my little friend, *Dulcinea*, high and dry and safe.

The night overtook me and soon it was dawn. The river was gray and drizzly like it was the second day out near the start of my trip. I watched the tows go by and realized that I wouldn't feel those waves under me for a while, nor would I smell the water, hear the sounds, or visit new people on a daily basis for some time. It would be back to that other world, away from this 8-mph world that so few know about.

Looking out over this great river, I thought of the things I did not do and the things I did; things I wished I had taken the time to do and things I did not take the time to do; things I was not brave enough to do and things I should have thought about a little more before I did them; the people who just passed in and out of my life and those who imprinted it with fire.

I wondered if I left with others as much as they left with me—the memories and the subtle and not-so-subtle changes that last forever.

As I sat waiting for my friend Tom who was going to give me a ride to get the truck with which I'd haul *Dulcinea* home, I reflected on the trip. I thought about how my boundaries were expanded, my vision made more clear. Yet there were many more questions to be answered, many more to ask. As much as it may seem, I have just touched the surface, like skippin' rocks down the Mississippi.

EPILOGUE

Ever Changing, Ever the Same

I wonder if the river I traveled will be the same river in the future. Things out there are changing so fast that I fear it will be much more difficult (if not impossible) for a future voyager to experience the same serendipity as I did. There is a spirit and a soul to the river that I'm afraid will disappear as Merle and his yellow kayak vanished into the mist.

I fear that new technology and new rules, while intended to improve efficiency and safety, will kill the spirit of helpfulness and cooperation on the river. Each rule and each added gadget by itself is only a small step, but taken together, they seem to further distance people from the river and from each other. At Cargo Carriers, they used computer models to help them string barges together with greater efficiency. Computers are also used more and more on the boats to tell the pilot how to run the boat, set the engine speed, and determine where in the river to position the boat based on engine temperature, fuel use, river current, wind, and other factors.

Some of the newer boats also transmit this information to the home office, even if the boat is in New Orleans and the office is in Pittsburgh. With the satellite positioning systems, there is no hiding in some backwater. The man at the bankside computer will know within feet where the boat is and what is going on at the same time as those on it.

The romanticism of past days of Mark Twain are rapidly being replaced by the cold technology of future days of Buck Rogers. When Mark Twain was a pilot, he had to memorize the river in both directions and intimately understand its twists and turns, even in the dark. Some day, the pilot may just get a voice mail message from a talking computer hundreds of miles away, telling him to watch out for that upcoming wing dam. Progress is nice, but it is sad to see a way of life change so rapidly. And I wonder what price we pay for being so advanced. Like George, the Yugoslavian oysterman in Empire who worked with cold, wet, bare hands rather than using gloves, I fear technology will make us lose the "feel" of the river.

The human landscape is changing, too.

In a phone call to an ol' river mate in Natchez, I learned that Steve Stevens died in the summer of 1994. With his passing went his riverman's dock that was there to serve the needs of those who used the river or just passed through. Now there are grandiose plans for the area by those who view the river only with curiosity and trivial pursuits, namely for the serious business of exchanging money for commerce—a dock for the casino boats. Rivermen can look elsewhere, as had been the case at Greenville and Vicksburg already.

About the time I heard about Steve, I had a conversation with Mike Rushing from Cape Girardeau, a sometime towboat operator and sometime captain of someone else's ship. He told me there had been some big-time talk of taking over that ninety-year tradition below Saint Louis, another riverman's hangout, Hoppie's. Some think this picturesque location should be put to a better and more valuable use as a docksite for another casino boat. That talk has died down a bit, but people in the Coast Guard tell me Hoppie is looking for a buyer—hopefully one who will keep it open as a riverman's dock.

I had just about lost all hope for the future of the river, when I stumbled across a book about the river's past. *Shantyboat* by the late Harlan Hubbard, gave me hope that the river could maintain its soul despite the many changes. It's about the trip Hubbard and his wife, Anna, made down the Ohio and Mississippi rivers from 1944 to 1950. At first, the book was just a good story of a river traveler—until they reached 1948 when they neared the Mississippi River junction at Cairo. Here their stories began to have a familiar ring to me—the flavor of an old friend lapping at the water line. There were not only familiar names of towns, bends and islands, but familiar stories of the people...some of the same charac-